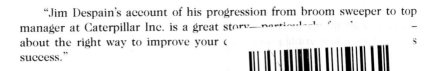

"Jim Despain's account of his progression from broom sweeper to top manager at Caterpillar Inc. is a great story—particularly ... about the right way to improve your (... s success."

D0711084

"Jim Despain pulls off this business memoir beautifully. It is a rare and honest look at what it was like for a low-level employee to struggle and overcome obstacles in a not-always-friendly corporate environment. Jim's climb up the ladder is inspiring. Start-up employees as well as executives should read this book carefully."

—ROBERT SLATER
Author, *Jack Welch and the GE Way*

"The cry for corporate integrity is greater today than ever before. ...*And Dignity for All* shows us how to succeed with integrity, not just succeed. It is a compelling case study of a wonderful journey toward individual transition and corporate transition."

—MARSHALL GOLDSMITH
Founding Director of the Financial Times Knowledge Dialogue
and the Alliance for Strategic Leadership and author
of 14 books, including *The Leader of the Future*
(a *BusinessWeek* best-seller)

"They say people can't change, but this book will convince you it's not true. I saw the Values Process described in this book change Jim and his team from autocratic managers to real leaders. And I saw their business improve far beyond anyone's expectations. This book proves what we know in our hearts—that trusting and respecting people makes good business sense."

—GERALD L. SHAHEEN
Group President, Caterpillar Inc.

"This is absolutely the most inspiring story about corporate leadership that I have read in the past 15 years! If you want to understand how to turn on employees and turn up profits, Jim Despain's real life journey from floor sweeper to vice president of a $20 billion company is a must read. Every chapter is filled with important insights for transforming any business into a great company. So refreshing. Almost makes life worth living."

—ERIC STEPHAN
BYU, Marriott School of Business
and author of *Powerful Leadership*

Praise for ...*And Dignity for All*

"When Jim Despain asked me to write a foreword for his book, ...*And Dignity for All*, I was thrilled. Why? I'm a big Jim Despain fan. You're going to love this book. What people want in leaders today, more than ever before, is integrity—walking their talk. ...*And Dignity for All* is all about integrity. This might very well be the best management book you ever read. I know it will help you unleash the power and potential of your human organization. Thanks, Jim."

—KEN BLANCHARD
Co-author, *The One Minute Manager*

"I highly recommend Jim Despain's book, ...*And Dignity for All*, to any-one who aspires to reach his or her dreams. It is an excellent story that clear-ly outlines how important it is to take risks, face your fears, and overcome any obstacles to reach success. This book allows readers to reflect on how they can transform their lives into something they never thought could be imaginable.

"Through my personal experience as a former high school teacher and as a leader in the United States Congress, I have learned to recognize the qualities of a great leader. While serving in these capacities, I have come to understand the truth behind the saying, 'leaders aren't born, they are made.' This message is conveyed throughout the book as Jim Despain tells a story about his transformational journey through life that helped him develop into a charismatic and effective leader. It is a story about how he worked his way up the ranks in a high-profile company named Caterpillar, always with steady focus and with fierce determination that allowed him to overcome any challenge that came his way. Furthermore, it shows how Jim Despain inspired his workforce to put aside their differences and trust one another in order to pursue a more efficient, positive working environment.

"It was encouraging to read about Jim growing up in a small mining town in Illinois. He never received a college degree, but still managed to develop into one of the more respected, inspirational leaders and role models within the Caterpillar organization. This book reinforced my belief that each indi-vidual is responsible for the outcome of their own future—that success isn't always handed to a person on a silver platter, but rather earned through hard work and determination.

"I am thankful Jim Despain shared his personal story so that others might have the chance to understand what it takes to be a successful leader and, above all, how to make any career aspiration come true."

—J. DENNIS HASTERT
Speaker of the House

"I met Jim and his management team during the deployment stage of their Common Values process. At first, I thought the effort was superficial and a 'program of the day' activity. I was wrong. There is no question this division accomplished an effective, almost unbelievable transformation. Their ability to maintain the gains from our work with them (or their Class A achievement) is clear evidence."

—JIM CORRELL
Chairman, Oliver Wight Americas

"...*And Dignity for All* is not only a compelling story, it is a blueprint for how to succeed in any business. Using the values process described in this book, we took a similar journey and achieved consistent, extraordinary performance. Whether you are in a product business or in a service business like we are, the job of leaders everywhere is to serve and honor people. When people feel good about themselves, each other, and their place of employment, performance always gets better."

—W. MICHAEL BRYANT
President and CEO, Methodist Health Services

"What an incredible book—a page turner! Jim Despain learned values-based leadership not by idealizing, but rather by experiencing what no longer works in business and inventing and implementing what does work. A must read for anyone attempting to deliver extraordinary results today."

—MICHAEL BASCH
Co-founder of FedEx and author of *CustomerCulture*

"Mr. Despain's book allows the reader to take himself/herself, the enterprise, far, far, far beyond the 'talk.' It allows the reader, should he/she have the moxie and the energy, to inculcate a system of organizational behavior that will (in actuality, not in theory) produce nothing less than outstanding organizational results.

"Beware: the practical application of the concepts contained in this book is not for the faint of heart. I dare say it will constitute the most challenging action you will have ever taken and, should you succeed, produce the greatest reward you have ever achieved."

—P. JOSEPH O'NEILL
President, G&D Transportation

...AND DIGNITY FOR ALL

ISBN 0-13-100532-4

FT Prentice Hall

FINANCIAL TIMES

In an increasingly competitive world, it is quality of thinking that gives an edge—an idea that opens new doors, a technique that solves a problem, or an insight that simply helps make sense of it all.

We work with leading authors in the various arenas of business and finance to bring cutting-edge thinking and best learning practice to a global market.

It is our goal to create world-class print publications and electronic products that give readers knowledge and understanding which can then be applied, whether studying or at work.

To find out more about our business products, you can visit us at www.ft-ph.com

Pearson Education

...And Dignity for All

Unlocking Greatness through Values-Based Leadership

James Despain
Jane Bodman Converse

An imprint of PEARSON EDUCATION
Upper Saddle River, NJ • New York • London • San Francisco • Toronto • Sydney
Tokyo • Singapore • Hong Kong • Cape Town • Madrid
Paris • Milan • Munich • Amsterdam

www.ft-ph.com

Library of Congress Cataloging-in-Publication Data

Despain, James.
   And diginity for all: unlocking the greatness through values-based leadership/ James
Despain, Jane Bodman Converse.
   p. cm.
   Includes bibliographical references.
   ISBN 0-13-100532-4
   1. Despain, Jim. 2. Caterpillar Inc.—Employees—Biography. 3. Executives—United
States—Biography. 4. Caterpillar Inc.—Management. 5. Executive ability. 6. Leadership.
I. Converse, Jane Bodman. II. Title.

HD9710.4.U62 D48 2003
338.7'629225'092—dc21
[B]   2002192753

Editorial/production supervision: *Kerry Reardon*
Cover design director: *Jerry Votta*
Cover design: *Anthony Gemmellaro*
Art director: *Gail Cocker-Bogusz*
Interior design: *Meg Van Arsdale*
Manufacturing manager: *Alexis Heydt-Long*
Manufacturing buyer: *Maura Zaldivar*
VP, executive editor: *Tim Moore*
Editorial assistant: *Allyson Kloss*
Marketing manager: *John Pierce*
Full-service production manager: *Anne R. Garcia*

 © 2003 by Pearson Education, Inc.
Publishing as Financial Times Prentice Hall
Upper Saddle River, NJ 07458

Financial Times Prentice Hall books are widely used by corporations
and government agencies for training, marketing, and resale.

For information regarding corporate and government bulk discounts please contact:
Corporate and Government Sales (800) 382-3419 or corpsales@pearsontechgroup.com

Printed in the United States of America
10   9   8   7   6   5   4   3   2   1

ISBN 0-13-100532-4

Pearson Education LTD.
Pearson Education Australia PTY, Limited
Pearson Education Singapore, Pte. Ltd.
Pearson Education North Asia Ltd.
Pearson Education Canada, Ltd.
Pearson Educación de Mexico, S.A. de C.V.
Pearson Education–Japan
Pearson Education Malaysia, Pte. Ltd.

Financial Times Prentice Hall Books

For more information, please go to www.ft-ph.com

Dr. Judith M. Bardwick
Seeking the Calm in the Storm: Managing Chaos in Your Business Life

Gerald R. Baron
Now Is Too Late: Survival in an Era of Instant News

Thomas L. Barton, William G. Shenkir, and Paul L. Walker
Making Enterprise Risk Management Pay Off: How Leading Companies Implement Risk Management

Michael Basch
CustomerCulture: How FedEx and Other Great Companies Put the Customer First Every Day

J. Stewart Black and Hal B. Gregersen
Leading Strategic Change: Breaking Through the Brain Barrier

Deirdre Breakenridge
Cyberbranding: Brand Building in the Digital Economy

Deirdre Breakenridge and Thomas J. DeLoughry
The New PR Toolkit: Strategies for Successful Media Relations

William C. Byham, Audrey B. Smith, and Matthew J. Paese
Grow Your Own Leaders: How to Identify, Develop, and Retain Leadership Talent

Jonathan Cagan and Craig M. Vogel
Creating Breakthrough Products: Innovation from Product Planning to Program Approval

David M. Carter and Darren Rovell
On the Ball: What You Can Learn About Business from Sports Leaders

Subir Chowdhury
Organization 21C: Someday All Organizations Will Lead this Way

Subir Chowdhury
The Talent Era: Achieving a High Return on Talent

Sherry Cooper
Ride the Wave: Taking Control in a Turbulent Financial Age

James W. Cortada
21st Century Business: Managing and Working in the New Digital Economy

James W. Cortada
Making the Information Society: Experience, Consequences, and Possibilities

Aswath Damodaran
The Dark Side of Valuation: Valuing Old Tech, New Tech, and New Economy Companies

Henry A. Davis and William W. Sihler
Financial Turnarounds: Preserving Enterprise Value

Ross Dawson
Living Networks: Leading Your Company, Customers, and Partners in the Hyper-connected Economy

Jim Despain and Jane Bodman Converse
And Dignity for All: Unlocking Greatness through Values-Based Leadership

CONTENTS

FOREWORD

When Jim Despain asked me to write a foreword for his book, *...And Dignity for All,* I was thrilled. Why? I'm a big Jim Despain fan. I really got to know Jim in 1995 when he came to present at the annual client conference that the Blanchard Companies hold every year. At this conference, Bob Logue, one of our sales consultants, and Don Carew, one of our founding consulting partners, invited Jim to share his learnings from the incredible culture change effort he was leading as vice president and general manager of one of the largest manufacturing facilities of Caterpillar Inc.—the Track-Type Tractors Division headquartered in East Peoria, Illinois.

Jim mesmerized the crowd not only with the magnitude of the changes they were attempting but also with his life story—the journey that brought him to the "right place at the right time." *...And Dignity for All* is an outgrowth of that speech and the follow-up talk Jim did by popular demand the next year at our 1996 client conference.

In many ways, *...And Dignity for All* is two books in one. First, it is a story of Jim Despain, an unlikely candidate for a senior executive position at one of the world's leading companies. He began his career as an hourly worker and ended it as corporate vice president. His determination, will to succeed, and openness to learning catapulted him into a situation that needed an enlightened leader. And what a journey it was. It was a journey from a command-and-control, self-serving leader to a supportive cheerleader who led by example, serving the vision and values of the human organization. It is a story about changing a corporate culture and, in the process, not only creating a very successful and profitable organization, but also changing people's lives. Let me set the context.

In the early 1990s, times were tough for the Track-Type Tractors Division, which Jim headed at Caterpillar. In spite of plant modernization, reengineering, reorganization, total quality management, and the list goes on, the company was suffering heavy losses. Employees were bitter and uneasy, returning to work without a contract from an eight-month strike. As Caterpillar's original plant, the Track-Type Tractors Division had the crustiest of cultures. Consistent with many human organizations, both inside and outside Caterpillar, people were not working together—purposely. Management was unknowingly teaching supervisors how not to work with hourly people, and union leadership was unknowingly teaching hourly employees how not to work with management.

Caterpillar was at a crossroads. Its markets were mature; the economy was slow; and its competitors were improving their quality while lowering their costs and their prices. Caterpillar had to change—the market, the competition, and the expectations of the customer demanded it.

Jim looked into the mirror and realized that he was as much a part of the problem as the solution. Jim's background had been one of command and control. The style he had been taught was to talk more than listen, provide answers rather than involve people in decision making, and be more concerned with who was right than with what was right. Yet he had a few role models over the years who suggested there was a different way. Those learnings bubbled to the surface as he realized that the missing link to improving the way things were done was in how people treated each other.

If the division was going to survive, it would have to establish a set of common values—shared beliefs with standards for behavior in the workplace—that would guide the way the company's employees interacted with each other. The first step was for Jim, together with his division's seven department managers, to establish a core set of operating values that could overcome all the obstacles they felt were undermining their performance as a division. With trust and mutual respect as the foundation, they established nine core values and the behaviors that reflected them.

That's when Don Carew and a team of consulting partners from the Blanchard Companies got involved and I was introduced to Jim. Jim knew that if values were to mean anything, the company's leaders would have to demonstrate and model those values in the way they worked with their people. This is where he saw our team fitting in—improving people first.

You're going to love this book. What people want in leaders today, more than ever before, is integrity—walking their talk. *...And Dignity for All* is all about integrity. It begins with the integrity journey of a man and ends with the integrity of an organization—one where people not only feel good about themselves, but produce good results. This might very well be the best management book you ever read. I know it will help you unleash the power and potential of your human organization.

Thanks, Jim.

—KEN BLANCHARD
Coauthor, *The One Minute Manager*
and *Leadership by the Book*

Acknowledgments

Caterpillar Track-Type Tractors Division

- To Bob Gordon and my department managers—for the genesis of the values idea and for working together to transform themselves and our business
- To the men and women in our plants and offices—who accepted and managed change and who now keep the values alive and strong as new challenges emerge and leaders come and go

Caterpillar Inc.

- To the executive office—for empowering their divisions and trusting us to deploy this new idea, one that some first thought was "soft" with low potential
- To our dealers and customers—who encouraged us and who have fostered the spread of values far beyond our walls

Converse Marketing

- To the talented people—who delivered communication plans and materials that facilitated change at Track-Type Tractors and who supported our work on this book

DespainConverse

- To our consulting team—who help other organizations create cultures of achievement where people find the dignity they seek, the information they need, and the freedom to make a difference
- To our clients—who take the values journey and discover that by giving dignity to all, they get bottom-line results

INTRODUCTION

I am not your typical senior executive. I don't have an MBA. I wasn't born with a silver spoon in my mouth. No, this is the story of someone with an unlikely resume for success. I was married when I was 16. I didn't go to college. What I learned, I learned on the job. I watched and I listened. I read and I asked. I tried and I failed. I learned and tried again.

This book is the story of a lifetime of experiences and the lessons I learned that enabled me to become a true leader of people. I began my career as a sweeper in a factory that makes the largest earthmoving equipment in the world. I ended it at the same company—a vice president of a $20 billion corporation. This story includes how we transformed a factory and an entire division into highly profitable leaders in our corporation and industry. It tells you how to do the same in whatever business you find yourself.

In the end, through my own experiences, achievements, and struggles, I discovered that values, defined as shared beliefs with standards for behavior in the workplace, are the key to succeeding in changing and challenging times. These values aren't a moralistic code based on personal or company ethics, although ethics are integral. Instead, they are a blueprint for creating a work environment that drives success because they provide people a context for their decisions, broad boundaries for their ideas, and more freedom to make a difference.

And what a difference people with values can make. The Track-Type Tractors Division of Caterpillar Inc. saw unprecedented improvement—improvement in everything from profit to employee satisfaction. And we did this without extraordinary capital investment, forced "right-sizing," product replacements or additions, new marketing strategies, or any other traditional idea. By establishing workplace values, we caused employees to feel an investment in the organization. We inspired rather than constrained and, in the process, created a high-performance organization.

This book is the story of the transformation of a man and the transformation of a business. Its purpose is to enable you to become a more effective leader and to shorten your journey by telling you what took me a lifetime to learn—that true leadership is very different from management. Leadership is about others and not about self. It is about trust and not about power. It is about producing results by creating cultures where people know it's okay to be unique and different, so they willingly take off their masks, express themselves, and do great things. Their clash of opposing ideas generates sparks that light the path to progress. My hope is that this book and my story will help unlock greatness for you.

—JIM DESPAIN

DEATH
OF THE DOG

*The measure of a man
is what he does with power.*

—PITTACUS

was born in Greenview, a coal mining town in central
Illinois, near the end of the Great Depression. Like the other
children of my community, I grew up understanding the values of Abraham Lincoln, who had made his home 20 miles away
in the state capital of Springfield and rode the circuit through
Greenview as an attorney. I also grew up understanding the importance of the company in my family's life. Just like the genes
that determined the color of my eyes and the squareness of
my jaw, the coal mining company influenced how I felt about
the world.

As a young person, my observations of my father in his work
and at home left lifelong impressions and influenced how I,
much later, approached my own work. My father and his father before him worked the mines—dirty, backbreaking work

that required a man to put his shoulder to the job and his faith in the Almighty. The life and livelihood of a miner depended on his ability to pry as much of the soft, black material out of the walls as quickly as he could. He couldn't chip out chunks too small—they would fall through the screening grid and be lost as part of his income. The chips couldn't be too large, or the company would be angry. One industrious young man decided to chip out a block of coal the size of the pit car. When the pit car was tipped on the scales, the large chunk broke the scales' springs. The weigher fired the miner on the spot. There was no room for creativity in the mines.

Persistence, commitment, and strength were essential to a miner's success. Tons of coal determined how well a company did in the marketplace. Slackers, whiners, and weaklings could keep the mine from making its quota. That meant less pay for the miners or the possibility of the company bringing in immigrant workers to replace them. There was no room for questioning the authority of the mine superintendent or the company. The men in Greenview knew how the miners of Godley and Carbon Hill had been fired upon for their insolence. They heard the story of the state militia searching the homes of miners in Braidwood. They feared the horrors of blacklisting, lockouts, and "scab" workers.

The mines themselves were dark, damp, dirty, and dangerous. The mules that pulled the cars were often stabled in the mine, adding animal stench to the coal dust that filled the air. The height of the shafts often was too short for a grown man to stand upright, so miners worked in stooped positions to chip out the coal. It was disagreeable work.

At the same time, the miner had to be keenly aware of what was going on around him. The mine was an unpredictable place. The possibility of collapsing or flooding shafts, fires, methanol explosions, or the silent seepage of poisonous gases into the mine made the miner keep his eyes and ears open, always listening and looking for any sign of danger. Every day the miners entered the shaft, they remembered the lessons of the Diamond Mine disaster, where melting snow poured into the shaft, drowning 74 workers. They never forgot the horror of the more recent Cherry Coal Mine disaster, where 259 men and

boys died nearly 500 feet below ground because somebody care-
lessly bumped into the open flame of an oil lamp while moving
a bale of hay to the mules' stable. It wasn't their own deaths the
miners feared, but the thought of leaving their wives and children alone and unsupported. How would their families survive
without the paycheck the company provided? Where would they
live if not in a company house?

The lessons men learned from the mines were simple: Break
the rules and you pay; make the most of your work time; be
careful, be cautious, be alert; keep busy to keep alive; carefully respect authority. Mixed with these lessons were the basic
values that were the heritage of the people of central Illinois:
dedication and commitment to the ideal; appreciation of the realities of your life; honesty and trustworthiness. These lessons
were the forces that molded the character of my father and
grandfather. These were the principles that my father applied
to me as I grew up. Ultimately, these values provided the lens
through which I would see people and organizations for most of
my life.

I saw these principles manifested in the expectations and
actions of my father. His parenting approach was a combination
of the obsession to honesty of Abe Lincoln and the demanding
obedience to authority of the mines. Early on I learned the consequences of testing his boundaries. Like many parents of the
times, my father believed in the proverb, spare the rod and spoil
the child. The original meaning of the saying instructed parents
to set direction and boundaries for children, much the same
way a shepherd used his rod or staff to guide his sheep. Most
parents of the time, however, believed the adage meant that
physical punishment was in the child's best interest. My father
was no different. His rules were simple and direct. Don't lie. Respect your elders. Do what you're told. Trouble in school means
double trouble at home. Push the limits and the consequences
will be severe. Breaking the rules resulted in swift and painful
punishment, a beating on the backside with my father's leather
belt or a switch cut from the cherry tree. He didn't worry about
how much the whipping hurt or marked my backside; he did
what was necessary to help me learn not to break the rules.

Enforcement of the rules was black and white. There were no gray areas. There were no negotiations, philosophical discussions, or instructive lectures. My father taught by simple and sometimes severe example. He once had a Dalmatian, a dog he loved. He trained it to be tenacious, aggressive, protective—a one-man dog. It often accompanied him to the local tavern, where it sat quietly and didn't move until my father was ready to leave. The two were inseparable. At home, he kept the animal chained up outside. In spite of being told not to go near him, one of my favorite daredevil pastimes was to tease the dog by running just beyond the length of its chain. Angered by the intrusion into his territory, he would lunge toward me only to be jerked back by the constraints of his chain. One day during summer vacation, a friend from school and I were playing the game. We ran past the dog over and over again, convulsing with laughter each time the chain snapped the animal back. But one time, my friend became a bit too confident and ran too close. With a menacing growl, the dog lunged again and just barely caught the side of her cheek. The bite wasn't deep, but it scared the daylights out of us. My mom was furious, but she was not the disciplinarian of the house. She sent me to my room, giving me time to contemplate the punishment I would receive from my father later.

But when my father came home that day, there was neither switch nor belt. Instead, he entered my room, grabbed me by the shirt collar, and dragged me to the doghouse. With shotgun in hand, he led the dog and me to the coal mine. There he told the dog to sit. As I watched, he took 20 paces, turned, and shot the dog in the head. I was horrified that my actions had caused this terrible death. The obvious lesson was clear: Break the rules, pay the price. The other, less obvious message was to protect and defend your family from harm, no matter what the sacrifice. My father and I never discussed the incident or the fatal punishment again, but the image would never leave my memory.

Like all children, I sought recognition from my parents, particularly from my father. As I grew older, I began to understand authority better. When orders were given, I learned to obey them—quickly, energetically, and completely. Unwavering obedience pleased my parents. I constantly sought ways to exceed their expectations. One summer night, as I lay in bed, I heard my father complaining about cleaning up the "windfall" pears that had been rotting on the ground. "I wish someone would just chop down that damn tree," I clearly heard my father say. Aha! This was something I could do. I knew where the hatchet was. I knew how to notch the trunk to fell the tree. I was a Boy Scout, and I had learned how to do these things. I was so excited by this opportunity to please my father, I could hardly sleep.

The next morning, I jumped out of bed as soon as I heard my father leave. Although surprised by my initiative, my mother never thought to question why I was up so early and why I wanted a big breakfast. But I knew—I had men's work to do today. I was going to impress my father by clearing away a nagging problem. With expert precision, I notched the trunk of the tree. Then I swung the ax over and over again until the tree leaned, trembled, and fell right where I wanted it. The impact of the tree hitting the ground rumbled through the air. Pleased and proud of my work, I savored a few moments of accomplishment, then set out to reduce the tree to a pile of firewood. As I raised the ax overhead to begin disassembling the tree, I was stopped by my mother's scream. Too horrified to explain her anger, she sent me to my room for the rest of the day. I was confused by her actions. Why was she sending me to my room? Why wasn't she proud of me? She had heard my father last night wishing the tree was gone. I granted that wish. Why wasn't my initiative rewarded? Perhaps my father would feel differently.

But my father did not feel differently. The pear tree provided a source of food for our family. The loss of the tree was like a loss of income. My initiative was foolish and had cost our family dearly. Instead of congratulations, I received a beating from my father I would never forget. But the pain of the switch was nothing compared to the pain I felt later when I realized what my decision had cost my family. I had literally taken food out of our mouths. I learned that decision-making and initiative could be risky and painful. I learned that orders needed to be direct, not inferred. I learned that good intentions were not enough. Decisions had to be right, and to be right they had to be exactly what the boss, in this case my father, wanted.

***

I attended the community schools of Greenview. I didn't study much, but I had a good memory that allowed me to "get by." School athletics gave me a chance to garner the recognition and glory I craved. They also gave me an outlet for my energy. Coal mining towns were rugged places. Greenview had as many bars as it did churches. Miners sat in the bars, drinking cold beers both in celebration that they had made it through another day and as an anesthetic to numb the reality that tomorrow they'd descend into the shaft all over again. Drink led to talk, and talk led to arguments. Arguments led to fights. The fights were not all that serious, more of an outlet for the miners to release tension. The boys of Greenview Community High School mimicked their fathers. Fights were just part of the recreational venue.

But I didn't like to fight. I ran from many. In spite of my size—I was well on my way to my eventual 6-foot 4-inch frame—I avoided conflict. I preferred sports as my release instead. I felt my best when I was wearing the black and red of the Greenview Bulldogs. I relished the opportunity to compete. The world of sports provided me with the recognition I craved and a deep appreciation of winning. Sports demonstrated the principles my father had taught me. The rules of engagement were pretty well defined. You knew when you had scored; you paid the consequences for breaking the rules. You defended your team like you did your family. You did your best to make your team successful. And you could easily tell whether your efforts delivered what the "authorities" (the coach and fans) wanted. You either won or you lost. Pretty clear-cut. I played baseball and basketball and ran track. I was good enough to be scouted by major colleges, but decided to get married instead. While young marriages were not unusual in that day and age, especially in our small coal mining town, my marriage was younger than most. I was 16 years old, and my wife, Gloria, was 15. I had nearly two years of high school to complete before graduation. And Gloria was pregnant with our first child.

Our first home as a married couple was a small trailer on Gloria's parents' property. It didn't even have a bathroom. We went to school, worked in the evenings and summers, and cared for our baby boy, Michael. It wasn't easy for either of us to finish high school, but we did. Following graduation, I joined the Air National Guard, then decided to seek employment at the great manufacturing plants of Peoria.

***

As I left high school, I carried with me the beliefs I had learned from the coal miners of Menard County and my family. I knew by now that life and work could be hard, even harsh. I expected fear and danger in the workplace, and I knew it was my job to prepare for it. I understood that I had to compete with others; and to compete well, I needed to give my best at all times. I knew my employer would be willing to replace me if I wasn't productive. Above all, I recognized my absolute responsibility to my young family and their well-being. I knew their comfort, security, and safety depended on my ability to succeed at work. I would not let them down.

2

PITCHIN' PENNIES

We work to become, not to acquire.

—ELBERT HUBBARD

America in the years following World War II was a country of hubris. "Stormy, husky, brawling…coarse and strong and cunning"—Carl Sandburg's words described not only the city of Chicago, but also the attitudes of the thousands of men running postwar American industries. Most of the bosses in the manufacturing plants had lived through the war. Whether they fought on the beaches of Normandy, built the airstrips of Guadalcanal, or stayed stateside to ensure the supply lines to the fronts, these men understood the power and responsibility of command. They knew as leaders they had to have a certain toughness, a bravery, an arrogance that made those they commanded fear the consequences of not obeying more than they feared the task itself. Without such blind obedience, men got hurt, even killed, and objectives were not achieved.

It was this military model, steel-cold and certain, that became the foundation of leadership for the CEO and the vice president, the supervisor and the foreman. They were in charge, and together—applying the leadership of sheer command—they would meet the pent-up demand of America and the world in the 1950s. Sandburg's poetry captures the souls of men like these: "Bragging and laughing that under his wrist is a pulse, and under his ribs, the heart of the people." These men knew they controlled more than their factories—they controlled the very lifeblood and fortunes of the men inside. Their authority remained unchallenged and their chain of command unbroken. The power of this command, after all, had just been demonstrated in America's dominance in the world over the last decade. And to question such authority was a sin, a breach of conduct, and terribly un-American. Even the great Douglas MacArthur was not immune from the propriety of command and control. His open disagreement with authority cost him his command and, many people thought, cost America a victory in Korea. No, breaking ranks, challenging command, and insubordination simply were not the right way to go in the 1950s. Everybody knew and accepted that.

The warhorses of industry had little trouble enforcing their command. After all, a great percentage of the men working under them also had military experience. When these workers had been soldiers, they learned the life-and-death importance of following orders. They understood and respected the position of leadership and comprehended the consequences of ignoring it. Those who were too young to have fought in World War II or Korea still were imprinted with the unspoken etiquette of the military. They knew that to get ahead you had to tow the line. Sure, there were strikes and work stoppages, but even then the workers deferred to the authority of the union leaders.

Company boss man or union boss man—it didn't matter: You knew the pecking order and you respected it. And the pecking order was clear and undisputed. The college boys, the sons and nephews of the company leaders, and the tough and seasoned company managers were the men who comprised industry's gentry. They wore gray flannel and blue pinstriped suits, starched white shirts, and ties bearing the colors of their alma maters. The company men were self-assured, confident that the workers below them feared their position and their power. To reinforce this mystique of position, company men did what many good military commanders had done in the war: intimidate, bully, and humiliate the troops into obedience and subservience. It was true, the workers did fear and respect the power of these men. But secretly in the privacy of their minds and hearts, the workers plotted ways to even up the score. They knew who controlled the machines, the rapidity of production, the speed of delivery, the firmness of deadlines. By manipulating any of these, the workers could intimidate, bully, and humiliate the company men back. Sure, there might be repercussions, like a lost raise or a day off without pay, but it was worth it to see a white-shirt get his comeuppance.

But the pecking order didn't stop with the chain of command. There was a pecking order among the workers themselves. There were the old-timers who knew the ropes and knew how to get away with stuff. There were the brown-nosers who had "friends in high places" and used this buddy system to get ahead. There were the streetwise city boys who had savvy and style, who could knock back the beers, flirt with the women, and make everybody feel like their pals. There were the country rubes, boys from the farms with Sunday school innocence that made them favorite targets for both practical jokes and misplaced blame when something went wrong. And there was another group of men who almost didn't count at all. These were the men with dark skins, who somehow had managed to get hired. It didn't matter that in 1954 the Supreme Court said segregation was illegal. Despite what the government said, white America still carried its old habits and thoughts about African Americans. In the factory, they still had not reached a status on par with their white counterparts. Finally, there were the women who worked in offices, cafeterias, and dispensaries. Even though they manufactured planes, artillery, boats, and all kinds of heavy equipment during the great war, now that the men were back, these women needed to take up their appropriate places in the world, return to duties associated with home, health, and charity. It was time for the girls to let the men get back to doing men's work. It was time, as Eisenhower said, "to get back to the business of business."

It was into this world that I came of my own free will. I came because I remembered how badly my father always wanted to work for Caterpillar, the big manufacturing company to the north, but couldn't because he had only a grade-school education. I came because my friends' fathers made good money at the company. I came because I was married with a young family to support. Yes, Caterpillar offered me lots of benefits besides good pay. It offered me a place to forge my future.

Perhaps, too, I could find something more at the company. I was still looking for evidence of my own self-worth. It seemed to be lacking, and my self-confidence was low. My feelings of insecurity were complex. Some of it had to do with my fear of authority, perhaps coming from my father's example. Some of it had to do with being born on the "wrong side of the tracks." The well-to-do people of Greenview lived on the south side. I was raised on the north side. And some of it had to do with choices I made that didn't necessarily fit with the conformity and conservatism of the 1950s. Certainly my marriage at a very early age opened me up to criticism.

I often felt out of place. My wife came from one of the "better" families of Greenview. My early capture of her heart and hand did not do much to endear me to my in-laws. I felt self-conscious with them. They treated me kindly—they were too Christian not to—but I interpreted their kindness as charity, a sort of *noblesse oblige* they conferred on me because I was a child of perhaps a lesser god, and by virtue of my marriage to their daughter, I was family. But I never felt I was like them. My speech was rough and unpolished. My grammar was inelegant and homespun. In spite of my hulking physique and towering frame, I felt small and insignificant around people like my in-laws. They were people of knowledge and position, who had a sophisticated and learned understanding of the world. How I longed to overcome my deficiencies. How I ached to become someone special. Someday, I vowed, I will speak like a parson, have the poise of a politician, and command the language like a professor. But that day was not today. Today I had to knuckle down and get back to basics. Today I had to start work on the shop floor. Today I would take a first step out of the chaos of my youth and begin to order my life as a man. Filled with anticipation and full-fledged fear, I went to a job interview at Caterpillar. "If only I could earn $100 a week," I thought to myself, "I would be able to buy everything I need."

***

In spite of my fears, I, like many others, wanted to work for Caterpillar. It had a great future. During the war, the manufacturing giant met every challenge thrown at it by the United States government, even though as many as 6,000 of its men were on military leave and women were staffing the machines. The company knew how to make great equipment. In fact, General Patton once commented that given the choice between tanks and the bulldozers Caterpillar made, he'd take bulldozers any day. With an endorsement like that and the pent-up demand for new machines and replacement parts that had been deferred during the war, the company had to build and expand just to keep up with all the work coming its way. And still there were more and more opportunities. The company's machines would be the equipment of choice for the St. Lawrence Seaway projects, building the great interstate highway system, and connecting the wilderness of Alaska to the other continental states. Business was so good, the company stock split two for one.

Although eager to make a good impression at this awesome manufacturer, I was bothered by self-doubt. As I sat across the desk from the interviewer, I felt my anxiety rising. This nervousness was not new. When I joined the Air National Guard after high school, I was sent to Lackland Air Force Base in Texas for three months of basic training. During the induction process, I was verbally abused by the drill sergeant to the extent that I broke out in hives. I felt as if my worst fears were being realized. My self-worth was completely destroyed. My upper body was so swollen from the allergic reaction that my shirt had to be cut off before my circulation was completely strangled. "Please," I thought to myself, "please don't let that happen now."

The personnel representative was nice enough. He kept asking me why I was so nervous. He encouraged me to relax. Even so, I could feel my pulse quicken and my muscles tense with each question. I wondered if he could see that I was sweating. I wondered if he noticed my hands were shaking. I wondered if I could make it though this interview. I even felt like running.

"When can you start, young man?" the personnel representative asked.

The words shattered through my anxiety. "Start, sir?" I stammered.

"Yeah, start work. That's what we're talking about, isn't it? You wanted a job here, didn't you?"

"Yes, yes, I can start right away," I answered.

"Great. Report for work Monday, third shift. Take this paperwork to my secretary. She'll get you all set."

That was it. I was hired. I was so relieved I didn't even think to ask what I was going to do. I had a job. That was something. And I had a job at one of America's best companies. That was something better. I was on my way. I was going to be somebody. I was an employee of the great earthmoving company.

By the time Monday rolled around, my excitement had turned to apprehension. I was scared to death. What if I messed up? What if I couldn't do the job? What if my supervisor didn't like me? As I thought about these questions on my hour-long drive to the company, I realized I was expendable. This giant company could replace me in the blink of an eye. I could be fired on the spot and nobody in the company would even notice. As this thought filtered through my mind, I came to the conclusion that I needed to understand the rules right away and never, never break them. I knew if you broke the rules, you paid the price. I had learned that lesson at a very early age. I couldn't afford that kind of consequence now. I would find a way always to fulfill the company's expectations and to mind my Ps and Qs with my boss.

***

Third shift—the graveyard shift, they called it. Work started at 11:18 P.M. and continued through dawn. The shop was cooler than during the day, but third-shifters had to fight the natural inclination to sleep. All through the night, steelworkers and fabricators transformed blocks and rods of metal and steel into equipment that could shape nature's hills, plains, and shores to meet man's needs. My job was not so significant as those who operated the drill presses and the lathes. My job was simple— sweep the floors, keep them clean of the gritty gray iron chips that sometimes flew and always trickled from the machinery. My tools were basic: two brooms. One was a push broom for big jobs. The other was a hand broom for corners and crevices. Even though my work was simple, I didn't mind the brooms. They gave me something to hang onto as I listened to the sounds of the shop. First, there was the constant grinding and humming of the machines. And frequently, the machines' rhythm was accented with harsh words and threats from the supervisors:

"You stupid SOB, why did you run that scrap?"

"If I catch you loafin' on the job one more time, your ass is out of here."

"What kind of a moron would let that machine malfunction? You'll pay for this one!"

The broom was a barrier when stuff like this was going on. It forced me to keep my eyes on the ground and avoid the "What are you looking at, boy? Get back to work" comments from supervisors. I heard these comments often.

And it wasn't just the supervisors who broke the rhythm. Among the workers themselves there seemed to be an underground war between those who stood together as a group to keep the company in line and those who wanted to help the company succeed.

"Hey, you brown-nose, don't push that machine beyond what we told you or you won't be walkin' for weeks."

"We don't cozy up to the company man around here. A guy could get hurt doing that."

"You better listen up, boy, or you might just find that cute little house you're renting in need of some major repairs, if you know what I mean."

"Hey, keep up that pace and we'll be losing jobs around here. You want that to happen? You want to put your buddies out of work?"

I found myself balancing lots of different voices. My father always told me to do the best I could. The people I worked with told me to toe the line and not do too much. The supervisor told me I'd better do what I was told. I had only been on the job a short while and already I had discovered the values and beliefs of my family, my friends, and my church weren't necessarily the rules of the world. The shop floor obviously wasn't Sunday school, and if you thought it was, you could get eaten alive. Still, something in my gut told me my mother's and father's words had to mean something. One thing I did know was that I would take care of my family. That meant I had to make a living. If that meant I had to make some adjustments in my thinking, so be it for now.

The supervisor soon rewarded me for my hard work and respectful attitude. I edged up the working ranks by becoming a wash tank operator. The work was dirty. My job was to take the oily, dusty parts, wash them in the tank, and blow them dry. I used an air hose to clear tapped-out holes in the parts. It wasn't the most glamorous job in the shop. Still, it was better than being a sweeper, and it was evidence that my approach to the company was the right way to go. Please the supervisor, that was the key to getting ahead. I worked hard and did a good job. Once again I was rewarded. This time, the supervisor offered me a real promotion—to a radial drill operator position.

In my observation, drill operators were people who exhibited real skills. That appealed to me. The operators' performance was measured on how much time it took to complete every movement needed to operate the machine. A perfect performance was 96.2 percent with a 3.8 percent allowance for lunch—a total of 100 percent. The measure re-ignited my competitive athletic spirit. It was like a track record that was meant to be broken. After a few weeks, I realized the 96.2 percent measure was easy to achieve. The time and motion studies that made up the basis for the measure somehow were inaccurate. If I operated at a perfect performance level (100 percent), I found I had time to loaf around, hide in the restroom, or just drink more coffee. When I asked the guys why they didn't do more, the answers were very clear, "Don't screw with the system. Increase production and you're giving in to the company. You're taking away jobs from other men. You're taking away overtime. A guy could get hurt doing that. A guy's family could get hurt too." So for a while I was content to follow the pack. Still, I heard my father's admonition: "If you're going to do a job, do it right." And there was that number, that 96.2 percent thing. It just stood out there like a long-jump record waiting to be challenged and broken.

It didn't take too long before that number started preying on my mind. I was better than that number, and I knew it. My father was right—why slack off? What was the satisfaction in that? It just wasn't right. After all, were we not taught in Sunday school to use our skills and abilities to the fullest? Wasn't that the point of the parable of the talents? It just wasn't right, no sir, it wasn't right to do less than your God-given abilities allowed. The conflict haunted me so much I contemplated quitting my job. But I thought of my foreman, who was a good and decent man. I didn't want to let him down or put him in a bind. Even with everyone working at "full capacity," there still was a production bottleneck on my machine line.

So I decided to test myself and the machine. I knew there were men in the plant who had threatened to break my legs if I did. I knew there were men who said they'd beat me senseless. I knew there were men who were watching to see if I crossed the line, ready to make me pay the price. But I couldn't help myself. There was that number and my abilities. There was my foreman, who had been so good to me. There were the lessons my mother and father taught me. And there also was my competitive spirit to push my own limitations.

Once I made the decision, I had no second thoughts. Something familiar started to happen to me. It was as if I was heading to just another athletic challenge. It wasn't a matter of overcoming the fear of physical harm from the radicals in the shop. Now it was time to put on my game face. Now it was time to focus on the task at hand. Now it was time to give my best effort. The competition didn't include those loudmouths in the shop. It was simply an event between me and what I could do. If victorious, I would prove something to myself. If I faltered, I would know I wasn't ready or worthy. The tenseness I felt that day was not fear of getting beat up—it was fear of not making my goal and the anticipation of shattering that production number to pieces. It was time to get going and get honest.

I checked the production requirements for the machine. I adjusted the tools. And then I pushed the machine. I made it perform. I broke 96.2 percent. I exceeded 100 percent. I'd done it. I'd worked to full capacity. I hadn't cheated myself or the company. Relieved at my accomplishment, my mind turned to more immediate matters. If I turned in the actual number, I was sure to upset some of my coworkers, maybe even the union steward or higher. That wouldn't be good for me or my young family. There was an easy way out, though, I decided. "I'll just turn in what everyone else does and run all I can. No one but me will ever know."

For a while, the ploy worked. But my boss knew something was going on and so did the rest of the guys. My foreman praised me for my performance. But my coworkers had the opposite reaction. They continued to threaten me and tried to coerce me into following the crowd. But it was too late. I knew what I could do and to do less wouldn't be honest, and I couldn't bring myself to be dishonest. Ultimately, my coworkers decided it wasn't worth their efforts to pummel my "lost soul." They didn't like what I was doing, but sometimes it paid off. I was always willing to apply my overage to the shortfalls of other guys. This live-and-let-live arrangement led to a quiet detante between the others and me. I could live with my work level, and my buddies could live with my occasional help. Both of us were quite satisfied with the situation.

Because of my performance, I was soon recommended for a promotion. This time I was working on engine blocks. Unlike my last position, this job required me to work with a team of men. We worked together, laughed together, and felt a sense of accomplishment in what we did. I liked the reinforcement I got from the other guys. It was a pretty good job except for one thing. Our group never did more than it had to. We never overshot production goals. We never hurried back to the job. We never pushed any records. It didn't matter how fast I worked. The next man in the process decided whether my pace continued or just gave him more time to do nothing. He never moved the block through any faster than usual.

Once again I struggled with the inner conflict. I wanted to excel like I did in the other job, but my performance was based on the efforts of the team. And this was a team that was interested in doing just enough to get by. As an athlete, this was a totally foreign experience for me. I'd never played for a team that didn't want to win. All the teams I played on wanted to win it all. In fact, in high school, my teammates and I were annoyed with a coach who just didn't have that fire in his belly. The coach was an okay guy, but he just couldn't execute. He didn't know how to use the talent of our team to win. I found this disgusting. If I hadn't loved the game so much, I would have quit. Even so, I never forgave the coach for not helping our team do what we were able. Now I was faced with the same situation. I resigned myself to the fact that my production would be the same as everyone else's. I hated that feeling.

Sometimes the guys would leave the machines and pitch pennies. With nothing else to do, I often joined them. One night, the foreman showed up. I was in a panic. I was certain I would be fired. But my buddies remained calm and continued pitching the pennies. When I finally looked up, I saw the foreman laughing. Even the boss didn't care much how our team performed as long as minimum production was achieved. I never reconciled myself to this attitude. Soon my chagrin turned to simple boredom. Doing six hours of work over an eight-hour period was absurd.

One night, my foreman and a maintenance foreman approached me. I never liked authority figures hanging around. I still wasn't comfortable with them, even though I was winning their praise and respect.

"Jim, you ever given any thought to what you want to do here?" my boss asked.

Taken aback by such a question, I looked up at the boss somewhat confused. "What?"

"Well, you know, ever thought about your future here, where you want to be in five years or so? You know, have you ever thought about your career?"

Lord knows I had plenty of time to think about my job and my future while I waited for work to come to my station. But this question came out of the blue. "Well, I haven't really thought about it all that much," I said. "But whatever job I get, I just want to do it well."

The two foremen chuckled. "That's good, Jim. We know you take pride in your work. But we think you got the makings of a good supervisor. We see how you work with the guys, how you take such an interest in gettin' the work out. We think you should sign up for the apprentice program. You know you need that to get into management," they explained.

Management! The word crashed into my mind. I wasn't sure I wanted that position. I wasn't sure I could be the authority figure. I wasn't sure I wanted to jeopardize my relationship with my buddies in this work group. Management. That was like crossing over to the enemy lines. But I didn't want to let on to my fears. "Well, I don't know much about the apprentice program," I finally answered, "but I do know I wouldn't be making the money I'm making now. You guys know I got a wife and two kids to support. And I'm not sure I can afford the eight bucks a month the company takes out of the check for tools and the toolbox. That's a lot of money for me right now."

"Hell, Jim, what you gonna do, work with these guys the rest of your life? C'mon, Jim, you know you're not happy here. Take a chance. Sure, it'll be tight for a while with your family, but think of where you can go. You know you ain't moving anywhere fast here. At least think about it, Jim, for chrissakes."

"Okay, okay, I'll talk to some of the other guys and let you know soon. I mean it, I will," I said. I couldn't believe I was saying those words. Why on God's green earth would I take a pay cut? My family was living hand to mouth right now. We couldn't afford this kind of change.

But before I knew it, I had signed up for the apprentice program. I had an uneasy feeling about my decision. I knew the real reason I made the choice was because I didn't want to let those foremen down. It was that authority thing again. I was afraid to fly in the face of those who had power over me. I couldn't disappoint them, so I couldn't say no.

The night after I made this decision, I couldn't sleep. I lay in bed, quietly thinking about what this all meant. I remembered the conflict on the shop floor. I remembered the distrust between boss and worker. I contemplated the lack of motivation of the workforce. I analyzed the attitudes of the boss men. I never really figured out the guys on the floor. They had a different view of work and accomplishment than I had. Maybe they had been there so long there wasn't any reason to push ahead.

Maybe the daily threats and berating made them dull and apathetic toward achievement. Maybe they never felt the pride I felt when I blasted a home run, hit a free throw, or cleared the hurdles ahead of everyone else. Even though I didn't understand the shop guys, I still felt akin to them. I wasn't sure I wanted to separate myself from this group.

Then there were the bosses. They had the power. They had the authority. They were important. The idea of being someone significant appealed to me. I let the word *management* roll off my tongue over and over again, as if I were trying to make it part of my vocabulary. Maybe management could be like being the captain of my basketball team. I allowed myself to imagine the perfect team. In my mind's eye I saw a group of people who worked together, who knew their positions and delivered peak performance effortlessly. I visualized a team of comers who were hungry for success and knew exactly what it meant. I allowed myself to indulge in that elusive feeling of being part of a team that's connected and energized, the kind of team that won't be denied. "This is what it would have felt like to be on a championship team," I mused. "Maybe I can do that. Maybe I can put together a team that feels that way." It didn't matter that in my reverie I confused athletic teams with work teams. In my mind, it was all the same.

As I drifted closer to sleep, I could see the faces of my old work buddies with me as their supervisor. But they weren't like the stern men on the shop floor. They were more like my mates on my old basketball team—proud, excited, and ready to do their part to make the team and the company successful. They were wearing dungarees and workshirts that matched, not because the company made them, but because they shared such a strong commitment to each other. "It could happen," I thought as I finally drifted off to sleep.

***

A compelling desire to work together on common goals, and the conflict it caused inside me when I didn't see it happening, made me begin to think about a better world and a better way. Why should workers and the company be at cross-purposes? I knew that something was wrong. Very wrong. The dissident seed was planted that would grow and emerge decades later when such conflict finally became crises. But for now, I was on top of the game and rewarded with a new opportunity. I was joining the company's apprentice program—the first and last advanced education I would ever receive.

THE SPECK
IN MY EYE

Failure is success if we learn from it.

—MALCOLM FORBES*

The opportunity to enter the apprentice program was a kind of second chance for me—another chance to pursue a higher level of education. "Not many people get a second chance in life," I thought. In fact, when I considered the people of my hometown and the harsh realities of life there, I wasn't sure many people got much of a chance at all. And even if they had a chance to do something better, make a change in their lives, reduce the hardships that faced them, I realized most people faltered because they didn't have the courage. It wasn't that the people I knew were weak-willed. After all, they put their lives on the line every time they entered the coal mine. But the coal

---

*Permission to use this quote granted from *The Forbes Book of Business Quotations*, Ted Goodman, editor, Black Dog and Leventhal Publishers, 1997, New York, NY.

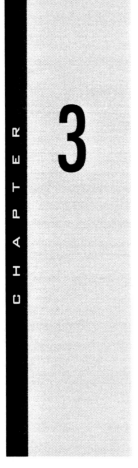

3

THE SPECK IN MY EYE

Failure is success if we learn from it.

—MALCOLM FORBES*

The opportunity to enter the apprentice program was a kind of second chance for me—another chance to pursue a higher level of education. "Not many people get a second chance in life," I thought. In fact, when I considered the people of my hometown and the harsh realities of life there, I wasn't sure many people got much of a chance at all. And even if they had a chance to do something better, make a change in their lives, reduce the hardships that faced them, I realized most people faltered because they didn't have the courage. It wasn't that the people I knew were weak-willed. After all, they put their lives on the line every time they entered the coal mine. But the coal

---

*Permission to use this quote granted from *The Forbes Book of Business Quotations*, Ted Goodman, editor, Black Dog and Leventhal Publishers, 1997, New York, NY.

mine offered at least the security of what was known and familiar. The future wasn't like that. Nor was a change in a career. These things created a different kind of anxiety. Where the coal mine's threat was real and physical, these other threats—the threat of change and the threat of the future—were slippery. You didn't feel these threats in your muscles. You felt them in the pit of your stomach. These pressures caused you to look at your abilities in a very different way. Do I know enough to succeed? Will I fit in a role and world different from the one I know? How do I deal with my competitors? What's to become of me if I fail? What will people think? How will I face my family if I don't succeed? These questions had to do with my sense of self-worth and were much more haunting to ponder.

I keenly felt the discomfort the questions provoked. I knew how to handle questions that challenged my physical strength and stamina in the work world. My large frame and my long association with sports had secured my confidence in factory work. But now I was being asked to do something different. I was being asked to lead and train people in the plant. In spite of my outward strength, for the first time I wrestled with the challenges of a major change in my life and future. I no longer was a worker who could rely on my physical prowess when all else failed. Now I had to be a thinking man, a planning man, a strategic man. I wondered why I had not paid more attention in school. I wished I had learned from the great generals—Julius Caesar, Hannibal, Napoleon, George Washington, Robert E. Lee, and Douglas MacArthur. I wished I knew their secrets for inspiring others. And I worried about my math skills. Supervisors dealt with budgets and figures and production ratios. Why hadn't I spent more time with my algebra book instead of my baseball glove? And then there was this whole human communication thing. My speech patterns and country grammar set me apart from the city boys and the college kids. Why hadn't someone impressed upon me the power of speech in leading people? Why hadn't I paid more attention to the eloquence of Lincoln's *Gettysburg Address* or Emily Dickinson's poetry?

Although it would have been easier and perhaps more self-satisfying to blame my town, or my teachers, or my parents for my deficits, I alone had made the choices that kept me out of college and left me far short of my potential. Now the company had given me a second chance. This time, I would stay focused. This time, I would apply the same discipline and rigor I had to my athletic training. In spite of my fears and anxieties, I decided to take the first great risk of my career. And oddly enough, the risk associated with my decision gave me a strange feeling of satisfaction and strength. I felt good about taking this risk. Maybe it was because the courage to decide set me apart from a lot of people. Maybe it was because my experience in athletics had taught me success was sweeter when the challenge was tougher. Maybe it was because the fear of failure in such a risk forced an unusual discipline and diligence on me. Simple decisions allowed a certain amount of slop in life. But tough decisions limited the margin for error, dared you not to lose concentration or become distracted. And in spite of my fear of authority and making mistakes, I liked making hard decisions. I liked taking risks. I liked going for broke.

And so I accepted my apprenticeship for management with an enthusiasm I had not felt since my high-school sports days. I recognized the opportunity for what it was—a chance to redeem my mistakes of hubris in high school. This time I was ready. No matter how boring the topics might be, I was determined to get something out of them. No matter how irrelevant the subject matter seemed to my own life, I vowed to find a way to relate it to my future. This time I accepted my role as student. I was privileged to receive this kind of instruction, and I accepted that privilege with both humility and purpose.

Oddly, once I had made my mind up about getting the most from my training, I found the material surprisingly interesting. The math was still the same math. The logic was still the same logic. But somehow since high school, the materials seemed to have grown and matured. Somehow this "stuff" teachers had to shove down my throat six years ago seemed strangely important. Somehow knowing this information made me stand just a little taller and speak with a little more confidence. The subject matter hadn't changed—I had. I started making connections between who I was, what I needed to know, and how that linked to achievement and worth. I now understood that not knowing wasn't a crime, but not being motivated to find out was lazy and stupid.

I learned the importance of intellectual challenge, of creating the connection between what others had discovered and the tasks I had to complete. I saw myself for the first time as part of a universe of knowledge and experience, science and humanity, intellect and emotion. And it finally dawned on me that the more I absorbed from the outside, the better I would be inside. From this singular apprenticeship experience grew an insatiable hunger to set priorities, to test hypotheses, to make things happen, to achieve more than what had been achieved before. I started to see that physical prowess was best when tempered with mental acuity and understanding of human nature. As I contemplated being a supervisor, I thought about how I would view my old coworkers. Would I see myself as separate and better than they were? Would I assume that becoming a manager had conferred upon me some special virtue? How would I get these people to follow me? How could I overcome the barriers that kept people from reaching their full potential, that kept them forever "pitchin' pennies"? Although I had subtly experienced the connection between human emotion and human achievement in athletics, the responsibility of being a coach and a leader started to clarify for me the wholeness of the individual. Physique, prowess, and strength were not the only things to look for in leaders. Attitude, character, enthusiasm, respect—these things too seemed to matter in achieving results.

From this point on, I started noticing more than just the outward physical attributes of people—how tall they were, the color of their skin, the loudness of their voice, the strength of their handshake. I looked for other things as well—enthusiasm, kindness, the desire to learn and grow. In a very small way, I began to discover that who people are deep inside affects a lot of what they choose to do in the workplace.

Although I was unaware of it at the time, my realization that people are distinctly human with their own thoughts, ideas, passions, and fears would later shape my solution to the most difficult business problem I would ever face. Even though the challenge was years away, a tiny seed of recognition had been planted. Over time, this seed would grow and wither and grow again as I experienced career transitions. But the seed was planted and would forever frame the conflicts I would encounter during my march to leadership. And no matter how hard I would try to ignore this concept of humanity in work, it would never leave me alone, sometimes waking me up in the middle of the night, sometimes interrupting my work during the day.

I enjoyed the classwork and the practical skills I was learning in the shop. My enthusiasm often brought good-humored derision from my fellow apprentices.

"Hey, Jimbo, you stayin' after school to clap teacher's erasers?"

"Hey, didn't they tell you that you don't get a grade for brown-nosing?"

"Slow down, buddy, you're makin' us look bad."

The taunts didn't much bother me. I volunteered to learn every machine on the shop floor. I questioned my instructor about any little thing that bothered me.

"Duggan," I would ask, "what happens if the calibration is off by, say, a tenth of a point?"

"Duggan, how does this look? Is the machining right? How could I do this better?"

"Duggan, how do you know when it's the guy and not the machine that's causing scrap?"

Duggan patiently answered all my questions, corrected my machining, and encouraged me. The old guys in the factory watched me as I rotated through the shop floor, learning machine after machine. Sometimes they would issue idle threats at us apprentices for working so hard. But usually, they didn't take the time to intimidate me or the others for pushing the equipment to capacity. They knew we were judged by our results. They let us rookies be, knowing some day we pups might be worn down by the organization too. The rough and eager enthusiasm we displayed in the shop would be tooled down to a smooth complacency over the next several years, they thought. Yes, the old guys understood the grinding forces of factory work and how sooner or later you just woke up one day and found your drive honed down to a simple resignation of routine in the shop and a severe stubbornness in your temperament not to let the company take anything more away from you, whether it was your money, your benefits, or the way you did your job. The seasoned workers watched and nodded. "Sooner or later," they thought, "one of these guys will be the 'boss man.' Then we'll have some lessons to teach him. Then he'll learn a thing or two about who runs this job." But for now they let us go about our business.

I watched my Ps and Qs pretty closely. I didn't want to fail. I made few mistakes. I lived for recognition and "atta boys" from my instructors. But one day, near the end of my shift, I was working on a mill cutter that broke without warning. A large piece of it broke the lens of my safety glasses, and much of the glass was imbedded in my eye. The glasses did their job—they saved my eye. But the incident, although it wasn't totally my fault, worried me more than the damage to my eye. "Darn," I thought, "things were going so well. I was making progress and now this. Duggan is going to be upset."

To my surprise, Duggan was truly concerned.

"What happened to you, Jim?" Duggan asked when he met me in first aid. The nurse was carefully picking pieces of my safety glasses out of my eye. The process was painfully slow and by the time she was done, I had missed my ride home to Greenview. The nurse taped a gauze patch over my eye and gave me final instructions in a stern, motherly voice. "You better take care of that eye, Jim, or you're gonna lose it. Don't take that patch off before the doctor says it's okay. And I want to see you back here every day until it's healed."

I assured the nurse I would comply.

"Gosh, Jim, you look a little bit like a pirate with that eye patch. Kind of a scary look, if you know what I mean," Duggan said, slapping me on the back.

Somehow I managed a weak smile.

"Don't worry about it, Jim," Duggan went on. "It could have been a lot worse. You could have lost the eye, maybe even your life. Yessir, I think you should consider yourself lucky. Jeez, look at the time. Why don't you come home with me for breakfast? My wife will make us some terrific bacon and eggs."

I was surprised at Duggan's offer. Based on my experiences on the shop floor so far, his behavior seemed way out of the ordinary. But I agreed and Duggan took me to his home. Mrs. Duggan treated me just as if I was family. She made a huge breakfast, kept our coffee cups steaming, and showed genuine concern about my accident. She knew about those machines and how dangerous they could be. She and Duggan knew several others who were hurt a lot worse than I. Some went on disability. "That could have been just terrible for you and your young family," she said. "It could have ruined your future. Thank God your injury is only what it is. Do you want more strawberry jam for your toast? My sister across the river makes it, and everyone swears it's just the closest thing to heaven."

"Don't you ride in a carpool, Jim?" Duggan asked after the coffee cups were emptied and the dishes cleared. "I know you missed your ride. I'm sure your wife's been wondering what happened to you. Your kids are probably worried too. Grab your coat and I'll take you home."

I was surprised by all this kindness. "Thank you, sir," I said humbly. "I know it's a long way. I insist on paying for gas."

Duggan laughed. "I don't want your money, Jim. Besides, if I keep you here, you'll eat me out of house and home."

I couldn't believe it. To Greenview and back was a 100-mile round trip that required close to three hours. Throughout the ride I contemplated Duggan's kindness. I hadn't seen this type of behavior since I started on the shop floor, and Duggan's charity touched me deeply. He never belittled or berated me for the accident. In fact, he and his wife had gone out of their way to minimize the incident and make me feel better. I kept trying to understand how this all fit together with what I had experienced at the company. It was unusual enough to puzzle me. I considered Duggan's kindness one of the most important lessons he had taught me. I made special mental note of his benevolence and how it made me want to achieve even more for him. This unusual enthusiasm was somewhat new for me. I spent some time thinking about why Duggan's concern had made me want to work harder and achieve more. "Why was this experience so different?" I asked myself. "And why is it making such a difference to me?"

As I contemplated what had happened, I realized that Duggan's kindness demonstrated his belief that I had some importance to the company. Duggan had shown me through his actions that I wasn't just an expendable piece of equipment that could be replaced when damaged. He valued me and what I did for the company. The realization that I had worth imprinted itself on my mind. At first, I didn't like this feeling. It was kind of squishy, goody-two-shoes, something my wife might like, but not me. But then I thought more about it. "Why do I now want to achieve more for this man Duggan?" And then I answered my own question. "Because he values what I do. He thinks I'm worth the extra effort." I tucked this thought away in the corner of my mind.

"This is the right way to be," I said to myself. "I will never forget Duggan."

***

Things went on as usual after my injury. Some days went well, some didn't. I lived for the days of perfect runs, when Duggan would tell me what a great job I had done. Each compliment I received reminded me of my contribution to the company. I liked having impact. I liked knowing I was making things better. Most of all, I liked knowing my skills and attitude made me a valuable person to the organization. I liked having worth among my peers.

Some days I ran scrap. I hated to run scrap and always wanted to know what I had done wrong. Duggan was always there, sometimes coaching and encouraging me, sometimes letting me have it for my mistakes. Most of the time, I made good runs. But at the company, your record was only as good as your last mistake. It didn't matter if you went months without running scrap—as soon as you did, you were back to square one and management's eyes were on you. Running scrap could ruin a guy's career if it happened at one of those times when management was scrutinizing the work on the floor or when the supervisor was in a bad mood. Every day I came to work, I thought to myself, "I want this to be a good day. I want to do well. I do not want my boss to be upset with me."

Overall, things were going pretty well for me and the rest of the apprentices. I felt good about my work, even though I had heard the company was slowing production. Orders had dropped off significantly. There were many comments about pent-up demand being met and the company facing an adjustment to work schedules. I had an inkling about what this meant, but business cycles were the things management worried about and workers didn't understand. My job was to run this machine and run it well. I continued to stretch my ability and the capacity of the machine.

One day I was assigned to an automatic turning machine in the shop and given the responsibility of running a high-priority job with a severe deadline. One of the company's suppliers had made an extraordinary effort to deliver a special run of iron. My job was to cut that raw iron into gear blanks. The finished parts made from these forgings were needed for products that were shut down in the field. Customers were waiting for these parts, and the company had promised them quick delivery. Here, I thought, was my big chance to show just how valuable I could be to the company. I set up the machine in record time and ran every single part in the lot. By anyone's standards, this was a major accomplishment, one that normally would have taken two or three shifts to complete. I was proud and pleased with what I had done and was sure my stellar performance would receive accolades from my instructor—perhaps even shop management—the next day. I went home that night excited. I could hardly sleep. In my mind's eye I could see Duggan and the shop managers congratulating me for the job I had done. I might even be considered an example for others. I was proud to be an apprentice.

I was really anxious to get to work the next day. I knew this was going to be a very good one. Trying to conceal my excitement, I forced myself to walk, not run, to my workstation. But as I approached my machine, panic overwhelmed me. There on the load of parts I had run the night before was the symbol of absolute shame for an apprentice—a scrap tag. My hands quivered as I read the tag. My work was .025 of an inch undersize, well below the finish grind dimension after heat treat. I knew I was in trouble. My haste to make a good impression had caused a terrible mistake in calibration. I had misread the micrometers used to measure the part. I felt small and worthless. I felt sick. And then things really went bad.

It wasn't Duggan or any of the other instructors who came to talk to me that day. It was the top manager of the building, the factory manager. My chest tightened as I saw him approach. My mouth was dry. My hands were almost dripping with sweat.

"Are you the stupid apprentice who ran this machine yesterday?"

Somehow I mumbled, "Yes sir, I am."

"Well, hotshot, your stupid mistake is going to lose this company customers. They were waiting on those gears and now it's gonna take weeks to replace them. And why? Because some punk—you—wants to run this machine like you're racin' in the Indy 500. What were you thinking, boy? Who in the hell were you trying to impress? I'll tell you what, son, you got us all into a mess it's going to be hard to climb out of. And I don't like being in that situation. You'll pay for this. I won't soon forget who screwed this up. From here on you'd better watch yourself, buddy, cause I'm going to be watching you—like a hawk. One more mistake and...."

The factory manager never finished his threat. He didn't have to. I knew what would come next. After the incident, I could hardly concentrate. My confidence was shot. My focus was blurred. I doubted every move I made. No one, not even Duggan, talked to me that day. I was like a leper. No one wanted to catch the disease called incompetence. Over time, I was able to resume my normal work attitude. But the conversation with the factory manager never left me. Even when I was feeling most confident on the job, the echo of his threats pulled me back. Maybe Duggan had been wrong. Maybe I wasn't so valuable to the company. Maybe I was truly expendable.

Soon rumors started circulating around the shop.

"Production's going in the toilet. Management's worried. Guys are going to be laid off. That's a fact; some people are going to have to be let go or we won't be profitable. I wonder who it'll be? I heard they were shutting down the apprentice program. Nah, they're cutting down the workforce in Building P. East Peoria's going to be hit and it's going to be hit hard. It doesn't make any sense, if you ask me. Why can't we just sell more equipment? People are building houses and roads all over the place."

Workers tiptoed around the plant like kids in a fun house, worried about what lurked around the next corner, but strangely happy to be inside. Still, I felt confident. I had done a good job and worked hard. Surely the company valued that in me. Maybe they would forget about the scrap. Other guys ran scrap. And besides, it would be silly to end the apprentice program now. We had only a few months left. Our measly salaries couldn't impact the company much. Although anxious, I let these thoughts bolster me each day as I entered the plant.

"Jim," Duggan called to me one day. "Gotta talk to you. Man to man."

Duggan pulled no punches. "Jim, we're laying people off and you're one of them. I tried to protect you from layoff by moving you to the weekly payroll. But the factory manager reminded me of that scrap you ran several weeks ago and he will not support you. I've gotta be honest with you, Jim. Some other apprentices will be moved to the weekly payroll. Sorry, pal. I know this is rough."

In my mind, I wanted to argue, "But I'm good at what I do. I haven't run as much scrap as the other guys in the apprentice program. I've got a family. I want to work here. I want this job." But my overwhelming fear of authority only made me stammer, "Thanks for being straight with me, Duggan. Any chance I'll be called back? How soon?"

"Sure, Jim, there's always that chance, but when? Your guess is as good as mine. I've seen these things before. Sometimes a couple of weeks, sometimes, well, a lot longer. Never know. But you're a good guy, Jim. You'll find something. Maybe even something closer to home. Maybe even something you'll like better. Now pack up your things and pick up your check. I really hope everything goes well for you, Jim." And with that, Duggan was gone.

"What happened to me?" I asked myself. "Why is the company treating me like this? I worked hard. I was interested. I did good work. One mistake and I'm done? What does this mean? Why does this happen?"

And then I heard my father's voice in my head, "Break the rules, son, and you pay the price."

**

I thought about the dog I had teased into breaking the rules and how my father had permanently punished the animal. I thought about the fruit tree I had cut down and how the guilt and pain lived with me through that first winter and then every winter thereafter. I thought about all the times I was punished in school for being late or having the wrong answer or not doing my homework. These reminders made my muscles tense and my confidence flinch as if I was about to receive a blow. One small mistake. One day of scrap. Break the rules. Pay the price. "I just forgot and now I'm paying for it. But I won't forget ever again," I said as I cleaned out my locker. And I would not.

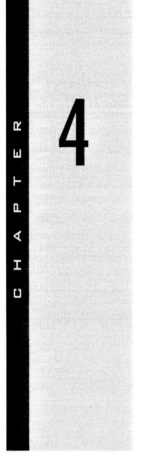

CHAPTER 4

BENCHED

The hardest work is to go idle.

—JEWISH PROVERB

I had a hard time fathoming the feeling that came from being released from my job, but I knew I had seen it somewhere before. I couldn't place it, and I was quite certain I had never experienced this peculiar emotion myself. Yet I knew I was acquainted with it. It seemed vaguely familiar. I searched my memory to find the link.

Laid off...out of work...pulled off the team. Benched... benched...benched! That's what it was like...being benched! I thought back to my basketball days. I remembered the guys who got benched—starters pulled out of the game. Asked to sit down. I remembered how players yanked from the line-up for poor performance looked as they headed for the sidelines—heads down, shoulders sagging, steps slow and deliberate. And I remembered

how the rest of us still on the court watched as the poor performers walked off. We tried to make our gazes nonchalant, but in reality, we stared at the back of their jerseys, watching intently as they were exiled from the team. We were torn between happiness at not being the ones singled out for poor performance and guilt that we put the game before our friendship with the outcast players. And then, just as the banished players caught their towels to wipe both the sweat and the humiliation off their faces, we would turn away, averting our eyes from theirs, knowing they would look up. We didn't want to catch their eyes. We didn't want to see their disappointment. We didn't want to look failure in the face. And we didn't want to give in to feeling sorry for them. After all, it wasn't our choice these players got sat down. They just weren't in the game this time. There would be other games. They might play then. But for now, those of us left on the court had to take care of business. We couldn't dwell on their misfortune.

My discovery startled me. "My God, I never knew they felt this way," I thought. "I never knew what it was like to be pulled away from something you want to be part of, to win at, to achieve." I felt my stomach tighten and a dull pain start at the back of my neck and then fully encompass my whole head. Physically, I was sick. Absolutely ill that I had been "benched" from the company program. The small shred of hope that I might get back on the team made it worse. When you were cut, you knew you were done. You were out. You could get on with your life. You had closure. But this layoff thing was weird and in lots of ways worse than being gone for good. It filled you with a longing for what you couldn't have. It crept into your thoughts when you were trying to do something else. It banged and rattled and echoed inside your head until you couldn't stand it anymore. You found yourself taking out your frustration on people not remotely connected with the company—the proverbial kicking-the-dog syndrome. I found myself cranky and short-tempered with my family and friends. I found myself uninterested and annoyed by the mundane tasks that filled my days. My family tiptoed around me; friends were cautious in talking with me; others just wanted to avoid me when I was down on my luck. My opinion of myself began to wane, and as my spirits sagged, worry spread throughout my family.

The needs of my young family, though, ultimately forced me out of my funk. The complex emotions associated with losing my job, even if it was "temporary," soon were replaced with a more basic urge—simple survival. I couldn't find work that would use the skills I had developed at the company. Besides, those skills were just painful reminders of my unwelcome hiatus. So I tried my hand at sales. Lots of young men were making a decent living selling insurance. It wasn't as physically challenging, and it left time for me to be a father and husband. And really, when I thought about it, insurance sales was the exact opposite of what I had been doing—a welcome and refreshing canyon between blue-collar and white-collar work. I hoped my new job would not only bring in the money my family needed, but also give me a new sense of myself. I hoped this different job would renew my spirit.

I started out my new career with high hopes, believing I could conquer this challenge with the same speed and decisiveness that had made me a star in high-school sports and had allowed me to move quickly up the rungs of the shop career ladder. But selling insurance was not like the other things I had done. It was more like chess than basketball. You had to constantly think of new approaches to the never-ending objections of the buyer. You had to be absolutely convincing to sell a product that brought no immediate gratification, couldn't be touched, couldn't be felt, and was useful only when things were terrible in life—car crashes, house fires, deaths. And I missed the sense of urgency of the shop, where there were always deadlines to be met, production quotas to reach, bottlenecks of work to overcome. An insurance career was not a good fit for me. The process was too slow and didn't allow me to do the one thing in work I really enjoyed—making quick decisions with some risk attached to them. The more I tried, the more annoyed I became. And the more annoyed I became, the harder it was to face my wife and kids—human reminders of my inability to make a living. My distress seeped into the household. Gloria told the kids to play outside or coaxed them to bed early to avoid my agitated state. In spite of my endless efforts, I wasn't able to meet the immediate needs of my family. Insurance sales commissions were based on a percent of premium paid. And during the start-up time, when an agent "builds his book," income was erratic and paltry. This job did not ease my worries. I didn't like quitting anything, but I had to put food on the table and pay the bills.

Finally I found a job in a construction equipment dealership in Springfield, 25 miles from home. It paid enough to keep my family just ahead of the bill collectors. I operated a welding machine that rebuilt rollers and idlers for track-type tractors. The job didn't offer me the variety or opportunity to learn like my apprenticeship had and wasn't financially and mentally as rewarding, but it served its purpose. It kept my family afloat, allowed me to keep up the mechanical skills I had learned on the shop floor, and most importantly kept me tuned in to what was going on with the industry. Although far from idyllic, the job made me feel in some control of my work life. And as my frustration eased at work, I found the tensions at home also relaxed. I thought it was simply the money and feeling secure that my family was safe. I somehow stood taller. My eyes were clearer, and although I was by no means jovial, I felt at least at peace. These things I hardly noticed. But Gloria and the rest of my family did indeed.

***

Months stretched on into a year. Finally, the recall came. I was going to be able to finish my apprenticeship and my life seemed back on track. I felt an overwhelming sense of relief. I'd be back in familiar surroundings and wouldn't live every week in panic that my family would have do without. To me, the recall was more than just a "back to work" invitation. It was a reaffirmation of my worth to the company. It was a sign that I had a future. It felt good to be called back into the fold. As I went back to the company that first day, my mood was festive, almost exuberant. It was hard to believe that more than a year had passed.

Work went well that day. I got back into the apprenticeship program and could feel the old rhythm of work returning. I met my usual group of buddies for the trip home and climbed in the driver's seat for the hour-and-a-half ride. We were particularly jovial—lots of back-slapping and horseplay as we left the plant. Our attitude was reminiscent of a group of 10-year-olds, scrambling in the fields, playing kick-the-can, dirty and sweaty from a hard day, full of life and full of laughter. Jokes and stories were the fare of the first part of the drive, always punctuated by deep, hearty laughter. But it had been a long, hard night at work. We were tired. By the time we reached the Salt Creek bridge, just a few miles north of Greenview, everyone in the car but me was sleeping. But then, just as the car crossed the bridge, I too fell asleep, sideswiping the bridge and damaging the right side of the car. Everyone was immediately jolted awake. I got the car stopped and my buddies pushed their way out, calling back to each other, "You all right?" There were minor bruises, but everyone was generally in good shape considering the accident's potential. "Whew, that was close," someone finally said. The rest of us nodded our heads and mumbled agreement. We were able to drive the car home that morning, and we all assured our families and friends that everything was okay. But I decided then and there I wouldn't be making that long drive much longer. I had just gotten back to work. Injury, illness, and tardiness couldn't be tolerated. The open road between the plant and Greenview created too large a margin for error. No, this time I was leaving nothing to chance. I would control what I could. And that meant I wasn't going to let remote highways that became impassable in winter, treacherous in rain, and hard to negotiate at night cheat me out of my career. That was it. We were moving to the city.

Gloria and I and our three children packed up our belongings and found a small bungalow in a community near the plant. It wasn't really the big city, but it was one of those suburbs that was the model of housing efficiency. Houses were close together, and many were identical, built to accommodate the booming growth of the American family in the 1950s and 1960s. They lined up on the street, one right after another, like the little green houses on the streets of a Monopoly board. Small sidewalks, accented with a sapling here and there, tied the neighborhood together. It was pleasant enough, but it wasn't Greenview.

The move created more than just convenience for our family. Unexpectedly, the change from country living to city living upset a sense of identity and security we had unconsciously enjoyed all our lives. People who'd never lived in a small town couldn't understand why we seemed a bit distant and shy, why we didn't enthusiastically partake in block parties and coffee klatches. How could I explain to these people that my wife and children missed hearing the long and soulful sound of the whistles of the freight trains as they neared the crossing? That sound, stretching out early in the morning as you wiped your eyes to begin the day and at night when you pulled cool, crisp sheets up to your chin, let you know the world was at peace. You strained your ears to hear the perfect rhythm of the freight cars passing over the crossing. The *chukka-chukka, chukka-chukka* sound the cars made when they passed over the crossing was somehow a sign that nature and industry were all right with each other. Falling asleep counting boxcars was a simple pleasure city people would never understand. There were dozens, no, hundreds of sounds that my family missed—sounds that provided direction in life.

And then there were the smells—things city people just didn't understand. The pungent and sweet smell of clover fields, the rich and earthy odor of cattle and manure, the scent of spring mud filled with a world of expectation—these smells signaled a balance in the world. There were the home smells—the yeasty smell of rising bread, the succulent aroma of fowl roasting in the oven when the boys had a good day hunting, and the fragrance of your mother's own sweat that you savored when you hugged her because you knew it was the result of her toil for those she loved. These common odors meant life was being lived, and lived right. They marked continuity and connection for the people of Greenview. And when they weren't there, I felt a certain insecurity, like being out of sync.

But most of all, my family and I missed the people of Greenview. People like Old Man Barnett, who ran the general store in town and had for as long as I could remember. Barnett never seemed to age, but he never seemed to have been young, either. He knew how your family was doing, knew when he could extend a little credit, and knew when sneaking a piece of penny candy to you was appropriate because last week you did a great job reciting your memory work in Sunday school. And then there were the farmers and the coal miners. Big tough men whose nicknames told their stories—my dad Dusty, Crank the mechanic, Swede the tall blond dairy farmer, and Chunk the miner who could lift huge pieces of coal and toss them effortlessly in the bins. Finally, there were the moms, dressed in calico house frocks and sporting worn but starched aprons, the pockets dusty with flour. These things made life predictable, simple, and secure. I never noticed these things as I went about daily life in Greenview, but when we left them behind it didn't take long to suffer pangs of withdrawal from the elements of Greenview that made life life. No one at work could understand why I was out of sorts from time to time. No one knew how the upheaval of leaving the only home I'd ever known affected my concentration and attitude. And in reality, no one really cared.

* * *

No matter how hard I tried to separate them, my personal life and professional life were inextricably linked. Trauma at work impacted my ability to care for and relate to my family. The reverse was also true. Our move to Peoria away from our hometown and familiar surroundings and the other pressures Gloria and I were feeling as young parents came silently to work with me each day. "I'll remember this when I am a supervisor," I said to myself. "I'll know more than just the names of people here. I'll care about them too."

5

UNJUST
REWARDS

How my achievements mock me!

—WILLIAM SHAKESPEARE*

In spite of my homesickness, I was happy to be back at Caterpillar. I finished the apprenticeship without incident and positioned myself to fill a supervisory position when one opened. But my first job after finishing the program was not in management. Instead, I was assigned as a machine operator in a new area, manufacturing automatic transmissions. My job was to learn all the machines and then teach others how to operate them efficiently. Although it wasn't a supervisory job per se, I found the opportunity acceptable. I was acting as sort of a teacher and coach. I enjoyed showing others how to run the equipment. I also felt satisfaction when one of my "pupils" did well. This was a new

---

*Permission to use this quote granted from *The Forbes Book of Business Quotations*, Ted Goodman, editor, Black Dog and Leventhal Publishers, 1997, New York, NY.

feeling for me. All my work life, my feelings of gratification came from what I accomplished, not what others did. I dismissed this feeling for others as just another measure of what I did individually. "If I wasn't a good teacher," I told myself, "they wouldn't have done so well." I could attribute my gratification only to the fact that my trainees' accomplishments reflected well on me. The connection between teachers, coaches, and leaders and the success of the people they mentor would not become important to me for many years.

After training the group, I fully expected to be promoted to management. But it didn't happen. I got put on a finish-turning machine instead. Granted, it was a complicated machine, but I still wasn't supervising others. It felt like going through all the conditioning and practice for playing baseball and then waiting and waiting and waiting because of inclement weather to play a game. I knew it wasn't a matter of *if* I would get to supervise, but *when*. And I was growing impatient with the waiting. In the meantime, I might as well show the company what I was made of. I might as well demonstrate that I was a "company man," willing to take a risk to make the company better.

So I spent my time studying the machine inside and out. I memorized every idiosyncrasy of the beast as if I were studying my basketball playbook. Finally, I felt comfortable that I had mastered the settings. One day a man I recognized as the union rep stopped by.

"Pretty damned impressive piece of equipment," he said.

"Sure is," I mumbled. Even though this guy wasn't management, he was a union official and had unusual power and influence. I still trembled inwardly at authority.

"You know this machine pretty well, huh? Seen you studying it all the time. That's good, wouldn't want you gettin' hurt or anything."

I just nodded.

"Thing about this machine," the rep continued, "is that even with all its bells and whistles, it still only runs 44 pieces per shift."

I wasn't following the man's logic. "Well," I said, "that's not exactly true. This thing can run twelve-and-a-half pieces per

hour. At 100 percent capacity, that means 100 pieces per shift."
I was confident of my math.

"You're not following me, buddy," the union man said. "And
I ain't impressed with your math. It's wrong. This thing can only
run 44 pieces per shift. Period. Ain't never run any more. Sometimes less, but never any more."

I must have looked a bit confused.

"Listen, stupid, let me spell it out for you in plain language.
If you're thinkin' of crankin' this thing up, think again. Doesn't
run more than 44 pieces per shift. A guy runnin' a machine
beyond that speed could get hurt, if you know what I mean. I
ain't talkin' so much about here in the shop. But you know,
strange things happen to guys who don't listen to what I say.
The boys don't like being pushed, and if they are, they might
feel inclined to push back a little. A man could get beaten up
pretty bad if he's not careful. Now let me tell you again, this machine runs 44 pieces per shift. No more. Understand this. I won't
tell you about this again. I'm warnin' you not to piss off the boys,
or you'll regret it. Get my picture?"

I nodded. The rep said, "That's a smart fella," turned around,
and left.

I continued to run the machine at 44 pieces per shift. But
at that rate a huge bottleneck developed. I didn't like being the
cause of inefficiency. I didn't like not working up to my potential. I knew the machine could run more; in fact, I was certain
of it. And besides, I had run equipment over what the shop workers said before and nothing had happened. Still, this wasn't
just my coworkers in the shop talking trash. This was a tough
union rep. He had the power to bring the blows down. But every
day that I looked at the stacked-up parts and read the reports
on past-due orders, I felt more and more compelled to take action. If I was going to be a supervisor some day, I was going to
have to stand up to hard-asses like him. Now was as good a time
as any to see what I could do.

Once again, I prepared. I studied the machine intently and
devised a checklist to make sure everything was in order before
I ran it. If I was going to take this risk, I wanted everything to
be perfect. I remembered when my enthusiasm for speed and

efficiency generated a heap of scrap and cost me a year layoff. Not this time. This attempt would be perfect.

On Monday afternoon, I came in to the shop ready to roll. I went through my checklist, not once, but three times, just to make sure. Then I let loose. I let the machine roll through the iron, finishing piece after piece. I watched carefully, making sure there was no scrap. My concentration was strict—I did not notice the other workers watching me coax my machine to do more and more. I wasn't aware of the whispers, and the curses, and the fists raised against me. I just kept running the machine. At the end of the shift I had completed not 100 pieces, but 144, almost one-and-a-half times what I thought the capacity of the machine was. Satisfied and exhausted, I noted my achievement in the production book.

The next day when I came to work, I found my machine surrounded by rough-looking workers, including the union rep. "Jim, that's your name, right? I think you made a mistake in that book," the union rep said. "No way that machine can run more than 44 pieces a shift."

I shifted my eyes away from the rep. "No mistake. I ran 144 pieces. I'm not going to lie about it."

"Not going to lie about it? You sure you ran 144 pieces, buddy? Are you absolutely sure? No way you could be wrong?"

"No, sir. I ran 144 pieces." I felt beads of sweat running down the back of my neck.

"Well then, Mr. Johnny-on-the-spot, I guess you and me and the boys need to have a little talk in the parking lot after shift. Maybe then your memory will be a little sharper."

"I'll be there," I said without thinking.

That day, I carefully checked my machine over. People with a grudge sometimes put shims under the fixtures or reset calibrations. If they couldn't get to you directly, they'd set you up for scrap. That way, management did the dirty work. I went through my checklist. Nothing wrong. So I ran the machine and, at the end of the shift, had completed 144 pieces again.

I knew this meant trouble, but it was too late now. I walked to my car resolutely, ready to give back whatever they wanted to dish out. I may have been a quiet man in the shop, but I was still in good shape, and my size was still an advantage. Even though I didn't participate much in scrappin' at the coal mines, I'd seen enough fights to know what to watch for. At 11:30 P.M. I stood my ground in the parking lot, clenching my fists and then opening them again, listening for trouble. Five minutes passed. I looked around. I could see the red tips of cigarettes leading people to their Fords and Chevys. Doors opened and closed, engines turned over, cars rumbled out of the parking lot. Ten minutes were gone and still no action. The lot was almost empty. My heart beat a little faster. "Maybe they're waiting until everyone's gone," I thought. "Maybe they want no witnesses." Two silhouettes approached me in the night. "This is it," I thought, but instead they suddenly turned left and headed for an old beat-up truck. The truck's engine moaned in the night; the headlights burned a soft yellow in the evening dust, and the truck puttered its way out of the lot. Fifteen minutes, then twenty. Nothing going on. Nobody left. Silence.

I closed my eyes for a minute, trying to listen for a hint in the darkness that something was coming. I heard nothing unusual. The chatter of machines on the third shift, the sounds of traffic a couple blocks away, the sharp bark of a dog wanting back in—nothing more. It was midnight and I was alone, absolutely alone. Taut and stretched from my anticipated conflict, my muscles relaxed in my clenched fists, then through the sinews and tendons of my calves and ankles. Finally, I felt my neck loosen and my jaw go limp. I looked around one last time, then looked up to stars in the sky. Without warning or explanation, a roaring peal of laughter came from deep within me. I laughed until I could laugh no more, not knowing exactly what was funny, but understanding I had conquered something that night in the parking lot.

***

The next day I walked into the shop with less confidence than I had felt the night before under the stars. Perhaps the union rep was toying with me, playing some kind of mind game. Maybe he was waiting to catch me when I least expected it. Maybe he was going to attack on a different front. I scrutinized my machine, certain that something had to have been tampered with. I went over the calibrations, the moving parts, and the electrical connections again and again. But there was no sign of the thugs. Feeling the tension across my shoulder blades, I ran the machine as usual. One hundred and forty-four pieces. I hit the mark again. This time when I wrote the number in the production book, I waited around to see if anyone would check my entry. But nobody did.

For weeks, then months, I ran the machine at capacity and wrote my production in the book. Every night I checked my car for mischief, and every day I examined my machine carefully. But there was never any trouble. Pretty soon I noticed the guys on the other two shifts were running the machine at 100 pieces. Production was picking up. Deadlines were being met. The shop had turned into a model of efficiency.

As I ran the machine, I thought to myself, "Well, the boss can't help to have noticed this. Look what I've done. Not only am I running this thing at 144 pieces, but the other workers are doing well too. They've gotta be thinkin' about a promotion for me. They gotta know that I'm ripe to be a supervisor." But no one ever talked to me about my promotion or about using what I learned during my apprenticeship to help the company.

At first, I thought I had done something wrong by running the machine so heavy. But my boss repeatedly told me what an asset I was to the shop. "Jimbo," he would say, "you're one hell of a worker. Wish I had a hunnert guys like you." I would mumble my thanks and go about my work.

One night, during a coffee break, I ran into one of my old buddies from Greenview. "John, long time no see," I offered.

"Hey, you old son of a gun, how you doin'? How's Gloria and the kids?"

"Good, John. How 'bout Mary and your family?"

We exchanged pleasantries, remembered with appropriate exaggeration key basketball games and memories of Greenview, and longed for the days when we used to play a game called King of the Mountain. John and I would go over to the cattle lot next door, climb up on top of a small tin building there, and step from it onto the backs of the cows standing nearby. Then we'd ride the cows around the lot, stepping from one cow's back to another's. Whoever could stay up the longest was crowned king. It was amazing we didn't get killed.

"Well, things sure have changed," John said. "But I can't complain. Got a good job, a handsome wife, and four sharp kids. Like my work. That's important, you know, 'specially when we're lookin' at another thirty or so years of it."

"Jeez, John, thirty more years in the shop?" I said incredulously. "Not me, man. I ain't hangin' around toolin' iron for the rest of my life. I'm going somewhere in this company."

"Says who?"

"Says me."

"You ain't going nowhere."

"Says who?" I asked, becoming more than a little annoyed.

"Says me and your boss," John laughed.

"What do you know about my boss?" I growled.

"Isn't your boss Big Stan?"

"Yeah, what of it?"

"Well, Big Stan and my boss eat lunch together every night. Me and my buddies sit within earshot. That way we know what's coming down the pike. The other night, we heard Big Stan braggin' to my boss about what a hell of a worker you are, Jimbo."

"Exactly my point. That's why I'm going somewhere. I proved myself, shown what I got. The boss worships the ground I walk on. He knows he couldn't do without me."

"Bingo, Jim boy. Big Stan knows that you're the one makin' that shop hum. He told my boss he ain't never seen anything like it. A big guy like you who keeps his mouth shut and does his job. Not only does his job but don't take nothin' offa the union. Man, you are a manager's dream. You make him look like God's gift to shop supervision."

"So what's your point?" I asked, this time without patience.

"Well, here's what Big Stan says to my boss. He says, 'Yessir, that Jimbo is one in a million. Makes me look good. Makes my life smooth as silk. I've never seen anybody who runs a machine like Jimbo. If I have anything to say about it, he's going to spend the rest of his life on that machine. Life is good with him in the shop, and I'm not lettin' anybody get him. Already had to block two attempts from other supers trying to steal him. But it ain't gonna happen, not while I'm around. No sirree.' That's what Big Stan said, Jim, I swear to God I heard him say just that. So you and me, buddy, we're bound to be workin' stiffs until it's time for the gold watch."

I wanted to scream curses at my friend. I wanted to grab him by the throat and squeeze the truth out him. I wanted to push him hard against my shoulder, like when we were kids, and tell him to take it back. I thought about wrestling him to the ground and thumping on his chest until he yelled "uncle" and admitted his lies. But I knew none of this was necessary. John and I had been friends for life. He had no reason to lie. He had nothing to gain from telling me about this conspiracy. So instead, I asked meekly, "Are you sure, John, are you sure it was me they were talking about? Are you sure you heard right?"

"Sorry, Jim, but that's what I heard, swear to God, that's just what I heard. Big Stan, well, he thinks as long as he's got you, he's got the gravy train. No man wants to give up the easy life. And face it, Jim, you make his life easy."

"Thanks, John," I said. "It was good talking to you. Say hello to Mary and the kids. We need to have a meal sometime together, huh? Maybe we could drive down home, or maybe you and Mary would like to see our new place."

"That would be great," John said, knowing I was deflated. "We'd like that." And then he walked out of the cafeteria, shaking his head.

I sat at the table, sipping what remained of my lukewarm coffee. I thought I heard laughter. I snapped my head around, expecting to see the union rep and workers who had threatened me the night I ran the machine at full capacity. But no one was there. I got up to go back to my machine. As I stood, I felt as if someone had landed a perfectly aimed blow to my stomach. Instinctively, I clutched my gut and then immediately realized my foolishness. But the pain didn't go away. It spread throughout my whole body, an agonizing and humiliating ache. I felt beaten and bruised by the very people I had wanted to join. I felt betrayed and humiliated and stupid. I felt like a sucker. And against my will, I found myself thinking, "The beating from the union thugs would have been so much easier to take."

***

Yes, breaking the rules and paying the price was bad. But not having rules or common understandings was much, much worse. My belief about what was fair and unfair was not shared by Stan and others here. This stunned and saddened me. As imperfect as it was, the black-and-white world of my father seemed a better way. I would remember this years later and help develop common understandings and post them on the walls in our factories and offices. But today, I was thinking only of myself. I felt abandoned and alone.

6 A Second Betrayal

*Nothing is more sad
than the death of an illusion.*

—Arthur Koestler

had not heard the legend of Sisyphus, a Greek man who so displeased the gods that Zeus sentenced him to never-ending penance. According to the myth, Sisyphus was forever condemned to push a boulder up the steep side of a mountain. Just as he was about to reach the top of the mountain, the boulder rolled back down. Sisyphus was forced to complete the task over and over. He had no hope of redemption or escape. Zeus had determined his fate, and that was how Sisyphus would spend the rest of his life.

Unlike Sisyphus, I had done nothing wrong. In fact, I had spent every working hour trying to please "the powers that be." While my actions and those of Sisyphus were on opposite ends of the moral spectrum, both of us were condemned to similar fates. No matter how good my work was, no matter how well I performed, no matter how quickly I completed my tasks, I was trapped forever on one side of the mountain. The exhilaration I once felt from a job well done turned into a dull realization that work was nothing more than a means to money. The special skills I had developed now seemed trite and mundane. Anybody could do what I did. I wasn't anything special. I had nothing special to give the company I thought would create a bright future. As the days and weeks and months under this cloud wore on, I found myself restless and cantankerous.

My rancor was made complete by the deeds of men outside the company. The Friendship VII mission took John Glenn to new heights of American achievement when he circled the earth three times. And then Scott Carpenter and Walter Schirra repeated the feat. John Kennedy hung tough and forced the Russians to remove missiles from Cuba. Engineers launched the Telstar communications satellite, the space probe Venus Mariner II, and the moon explorer Ranger IV. Mickey Mantle, Willie Mays, Don Drysdale, and Maury Willis made baseball history. On the basketball court, Wilt "the Stilt" Chamberlain, Jerry West, Oscar Robertson, and Bill Russell broke records and forever changed the game. Everywhere I looked, I saw men who were free to realize their dreams. Yet here I was, a prisoner in the company I so admired.

For the first time in my life, I felt oppressed. Someone was keeping me from realizing my full potential at the company. Someone had control over me, and I could not get loose. I began to understand how a man held back became resentful. I saw the world through angry and anxious eyes. Anger because I was held back, anxious because I was always on the lookout for an opportunity to escape. I often ran my machinery without thinking, daydreaming about what might have been and who I might have become. I dreamed about myself as a leader—proud, fair, strong. I contemplated the team I would have built—enthusiastic, intelligent, innovative. I thought of the results I would have produced—efficient, effective, excellent. These things were on my mind, day in and day out. It helped pass the time. I was in the middle of one of these reveries when a voice I knew from the past interrupted.

"Hey, Jim, what do you say we get the hell out of here?" my old friend Mike asked.

"It's not even close to shift change. What are you talking about?" I responded.

"Ain't talking about no 15-minute smoke break. I'm talking about for good. What do you think?"

"C'mon, you know better than that. I've got a family to support. I need this job."

"That's where you're wrong, old buddy. You need a job, but not this one. You need to work, but not here. Me and a couple of other guys are going to work in a small shop in East Peoria. We're going to help it grow. You might even be able to invest in it if you want."

"Mike, you know I don't have that kind of scratch. I need this job. I need to feed my family. I have responsibilities. I have to stay here."

"All right, if you aren't interested in making a bushel of money and getting the hell out of this prison..."

"What do you mean, getting out of this prison?" My curiosity was piqued.

"I mean getting the hell out of this place," Mike said. "I mean starting our own shop. I mean being our own bosses. I mean not having to check in every time we need to take a whiz or blow our noses. I mean making as much money as we want without any quotas, contracts, and timecards. And if we want to take a day off to go hunting or something, we just have to ask ourselves."

"I told you, Mike, I got no money to invest," I said sadly.

"Well, maybe you would consider workin' for us. You could work in the shop or maybe even manage. Hell, we don't care. We know a good man when we see one, and you're a good one. You're the kind of guy who gets things done. We need that kind of man, Jimbo. Think about it. I'll get back to you at the end of the week."

I felt something inside of me reawakening. It was a strange feeling. Sort of like hope, but different. "Someone thinks I'm worth stealing from this company," I told myself. "Someone wants me to be part of their team. They think I have something to offer.

They think I'm good. They think I'll help them succeed." The feeling changed the direction of my thoughts. My mind meandered down all kinds of roads to glory. I'd run the best tool and die shop in the state—no, in the country, hell, in the world. I felt myself standing a little taller, acting a little cockier. Something had changed. It was quite simple. Someone showed me I was appreciated. Someone said I had talent. Someone felt I was a guy who was going places. Someone wanted to take a risk on my abilities. What an incredible feeling! I tasted freedom. I tasted achievement. I felt alive again.

Of course, I had to consider the salary. I might be able to come down some. My family had lived with setbacks before; they could again. But I wanted to be sure I could navigate, or at least help steer, my future. I wanted to know I could advance and grow. I wanted to be my own man, to lead the way I knew how. I wanted to drive achievement. I wanted to make a difference. I wanted "the powers that be" to get off my back and let me do what I was able. I was convinced that would never happen at the company. But maybe in this new place, maybe with people who were like me, who understood who I was and where I came from, it could. Maybe here I would be able to stretch and grow and create, and my coworkers would understand and appreciate what kind of man, what kind of competitor I was. They would have to know—they came from the same place I did. The more I thought about the possibilities, the more excited I became. The new horizon Mike offered me was so appealing I worried it might not be real. What if he changed his mind? What if he couldn't find a place for me? I was a like a man dying of thirst with a glass of water held just beyond my reach. I counted the days, waiting for the week to be over. Finally, it was. I watched for Mike all day. Late in the afternoon, he showed up.

"So, Jimbo," Mike asked, "you ready to move on?"

"What d'ya want me to do and what about the pay?" I tried not to sound too anxious.

"Well, we think we'd hire you in as our tool and die manager at about the salary you're making now. You'd be in charge of three or four other guys, and you'd do some tool and die work yourself. So you in?"

"Hmmm, sounds pretty tempting," I said, trying to keep my poker face. "You mind if Gloria and I talk tonight and I call you in the morning?" Inside my head, I was thinking, "Please don't let him think I'm blowing him off. Please let him believe I'm a good businessman who thinks things through."

"Yeah, sure," Mike said. "It's nice to include the wife in these decisions. Gimme a call tomorrow morning. Here's my number."

Skyrockets went off in my head. My pulse quickened, and my heart started pounding as if I was chugging once more for home plate. I felt alive again. That night I went home and told my family about this new opportunity. I did not talk about the risk of a start-up company or the conflicts inherent in small enterprises. I wanted no objections to the decision I had already made. Instead, I explained why this move made sense for my career, how I could test the skills I'd learned in my apprenticeship, how I would lead the company to success. I wanted no one to foil my plans to escape my current dead-end situation. I wanted no one to find security or purpose in my oppression. I wanted no one to see my boss—a tyrant in my mind—as my protector. I wanted to be free to grow, to change, to excel.

For the past several months, I had had a hard time sleeping. My rest was disturbed by visions of my supervisor—holding me down, keeping me back, blocking me at every escape route. No matter how hard I tried those sleepless nights, I could not find a way out. Tonight, the insomnia returned, but for a different reason. Feelings of liberation and hope sent my mind in a hundred different directions. I could see a myriad of ways I was free. I wanted to sleep. Sleep would make the night pass quickly and the phone call I longed to place come sooner. But I couldn't sleep. My mind was alert with possibilities and pride. I lay in the darkness, eyes wide open, contemplating my future. I listened for the hourly chime, as the hall clock's hands traveled slowly through the night. I stared at the curtains, waiting for the first light of dawn. When the sun was barely up, I rose, ate breakfast alone, and paced until a respectable hour for calling Mike came. I dialed the number carefully and waited for the ring.

After three rings, a male voice answered, "Yeah?"

I got nervous. Maybe I called too early. Too late now. "Mike, that you?" I asked.

"Yeah, it's me, who's this?"

"Jim. It's Jim. Did I wake you up?" I asked cautiously.

"Nah, nah. Sorry, Jim, didn't recognize your voice. So, buddy, did you make a decision? You comin' on board?"

"You bet," I said, trying not to sound overanxious.

"Well, that's just great, Jim, that's great. You know where the shop is? Why don't you meet me there in an hour? We'll get things started."

"I'll be there," I said. "Lookin' forward to it."

"Me too, Jim, me too," Mike said. "See ya later." And with that, Mike hung up.

***

I enjoyed working in the small tool and die shop. I was able to use my skills more freely, and finally I had made it to a leadership position. I worked hard and so did my group. I felt a sense of pride and accomplishment, especially since my salary now included a commission for new business. The commission wasn't much, but it was symbolic for me of my success. I worked harder and harder to make sure the bonus would be as significant as possible.

In a few months, Mike and some of the other original managers of the shop left to start their own business. I had no money to invest, so I stayed behind and was immediately promoted to plant manager.

During the weeks and then months of my new responsibility, I cherished the feeling of total accountability. Although not totally prepared, it didn't take long for my leadership ability to surface. The company results improved, and George, the organization's president, rewarded me with both praise and perks. George gave me a company car and a gas allowance.

Sales continued to increase, and my commission continued to grow. Most of the accounts were bread-and-butter work, the stuff that kept the company going. Finally, a chance for a significant piece of work came the company's way. I jumped on the opportunity. I did my homework. I negotiated with the account people. I worked as hard as I ever had.

I felt I was making a significant contribution to the company. George and I held strategy meetings on the development of the account on a regular basis.

"Boy," I said, "I sure hope we get this account. That commission would look great on my paycheck."

"Your paycheck?" George asked. "I don't think so, since I've done most of the work."

I was stunned, but I could see from the look on George's face that he wasn't kidding. I had been guaranteed a percentage of all new business, no matter who placed it. The betrayal was double. Not only was George ignoring all of my hard work, but he was also going back on a promise. I fell silent, knowing now was not the time to argue.

Somehow the scene, played over and over in my thoughts, conjured up a feeling vaguely familiar. It was almost the same feeling I had felt when I was working for Big Stan, the boss who would never promote me. The circumstances were different, but the impact was the same. These bosses were using me. They knew I thrived on praise. They knew I was a dedicated man who never purposely used my size to get what I wanted. They knew my greatest pride was in my work, not in my salary, not in my benefits. I lived on achievement. They knew no matter how they treated me, I wouldn't let them down. They knew I had created my own golden "handcuffs"—my absolute dedication to excellence. Then they preyed on me. But their attacks were more sinister. They never showed open aggression. Instead, they used a sort of guerrilla warfare on me. They passively refused me promotions. They passively ignored delivering on the promises they had made as the stakes increased.

From that moment of epiphany, I looked at myself and my bosses in an entirely different light. I began to believe that bosses, by their very nature, always placed their own self-centered interests above those of the workers. Their success was determined by the culminated efforts of many people. And their success was measured by power, profits, and position. Any time they shared that with the workers, they diminished their sense of worth. Giving up power meant giving up control. How could you be a successful boss without control? If they gave up profits like my commission, their own salaries might be smaller. How could you be successful if your workers' salaries were growing faster than your own? If you gave up position, you gave up territory. Partnerships, stock, partial ownership of the company—all these diminished the size of your turf. How could you be judged a successful boss if you were shrinking your own dominion? These bosses were smart. They promised and teased but only had to deliver when it fit their purposes. This kind of boss–worker relationship was like playing poker with somebody who had all the aces up his sleeve. No matter what, the worker could never win.

This dismal realization made me understand that to advance my career, I might have to jump from place to place, edging my way up the ladder with each career move. I wasn't certain I could trust any boss, really. They were all sweet talk in the beginning. "Jim, you're the best worker we've ever seen." "Jim, we can't do without you." "Jim, you're the kind of man we've been looking for." But when I proved them right, they withheld the rewards they promised or kept me back. I couldn't fight them on their own turf. The only way I could fight back was to create a void in their organization. It felt callous and hard, but I had learned that flattery for good work was lulling me into a complacency that kept me from what I wanted.

So I quit. George wanted to know why I was leaving. I tried to explain, but he didn't get it. He was angry.

"I made you, Jim. I gave you a leadership position you never had. I let you do things you never did before. I let you sit at the table with the big boys," George argued.

"It's not that, George. It's about trust. It's about doing what you said you'd do. It's about supporting my work and where I want to go," I answered.

"What the hell are you talking about, Jim? I did everything I said I would, didn't I?" I was flabbergasted that George didn't remember the promised commissions.

"George, look, I'm tired of arguing with you. I'm leaving, and that's it. I appreciate what you've done for me, but it's time for me to do more."

"Well, you ungrateful SOB. Go on, get the hell out of here. I'm tired of your whining about commissions. If you wanna know the truth, I'm glad you're getting out. You do good work, Jim, but you know you've been a big pain in the ass. Always wantin' more for your workers. Jeez, Jim, they're just die-makers, you know. They ain't astronauts. You're some kind of supervisor, Jim. Maybe in your next job you'll realize your role is to make money for the boss, not the workers on the line. You're management, for chrissakes, Jim. When are you going to start actin' like it?"

The words slapped me hard. Now, more than ever, I knew I had to leave. I was a good manager. I treated people right. And when I did, they produced wonderful results. But George was telling me that wasn't how it was supposed to be. I knew George was wrong. I couldn't lead like that. I just couldn't. I smiled sadly, shook my head, and left.

***

I would take my skills and knowledge elsewhere, with the satisfaction of knowing that when I left, the company would at least suffer a temporary setback as they spent time finding someone to replace me and teaching that person everything I carried in my head. It made me sad to lose my naïve belief in the goodness of the bosses I had trusted. It hurt me on a level I could not explain. But the time had come to look out for myself. The time had come to demand respect for who I was and what I could accomplish. The time had come to take charge of my own destiny. The time had come to make sure the advantage was mine and not the boss's as I plotted my career.

7

THE PIANO
THAT PLAYED

Trust people and they will be true to you.
Treat them greatly and they will
show themselves great.

—RALPH WALDO EMERSON

Armed with new confidence in my leadership abilities, I called Caterpillar to see if the company would take me back. I reviewed my background: the completed apprenticeship plus two years of outside management experience, including my move to plant manager in the small job shop. The best the company could do for me, however, was an hourly position on third shift. I preferred working for the company, but I didn't want to start completely over again. I refused the offer and accepted a job as a quality technician at the company's local competitor. I felt a little disloyal about taking the position, but the company didn't seem to mind. After the last two encounters with Big Stan and George, I was making sure that I, not someone else, had control of my career and destiny. The competitor was a successful company, and experience within this organization certainly would support my career ambitions. I jokingly let my old shop buddies from the company know I would be working for a competitor and they'd better watch out, because I was going to come after them.

Shortly thereafter, I got a phone call at home from the manager of planning and tooling at the plant.

"Jim, I just heard you're going to work for the local competitor. Is that right?"

"Yeah," I said. "I'm going be working in quality. It's a good job. A little travel, and a real opportunity."

"What are you thinkin', Jim?" the manager asked. "Why didn't you call us? You know we always thought a lot of you and your work."

"Yeah, that's why you offered me an entry-level job," I thought to myself sarcastically, but instead I answered, "Well, I tried to get back in, but all they offered me was hourly third shift. I want to stay in management."

"Okay, so someone in personnel doesn't know your situation. If I can get you a better job than what you got with the competitor, will you come back?"

I had to think. Was this another one of those boss tricks? Maybe, but at least now I was prepared for what might be coming. "Yeah, you know, I think I would," I finally answered. "I've always respected the company, and you could convince me to come back if I can be a supervisor." I was a bit astounded by my own brashness. But I wasn't going to get taken again. If I had to be brash and stubborn to create my own future, so be it.

Later that day the phone rang again. It was the manager.

"Okay, how 'bout this, Jim? I got a job for you as a salaried employee—a desk job, Jim. You can do paperwork and, who knows, maybe another opportunity for supervisor will show up soon."

"It's a deal," I said without thinking. The phone call was significant for me. I'd waited a long time and gone down some unexpected paths, but now I was finally making the change I had contemplated so many, many months ago. I was leaving the world of the company hourly worker at last and was getting closer to the challenging, hard-hitting world of management.

The new job was far from management, though. It was a staff function in material control. Electronic tracking was not yet used, so my tasks were manual. I sat in an area with other salaried people who did the same work. As I learned the job, I was amazed at how quickly I could get through the paperwork. Yet as I looked to my left and right, the more experienced people were taking their time. Soon people began to notice that I was done with my work long before the workday was over.

"Jim," one of my colleagues finally said, "I know you're used to the production deadlines on the shop floor. I know there was always pressure to complete work by a certain time. But Jim, this isn't the shop floor. This is office work. There's no pressure here, man. Take your time, kick back a little. There's no hurry."

I was astounded. Here I was in the office and I was hearing the same slacker talk I had heard on the shop floor. Granted, I wasn't threatened, but I didn't think I was winning any popularity contests with my coworkers, either. Still, I didn't change. I continued to work to my capacity. A few weeks later, my supervisor told me they were going to add another person to my records.

"We're changing our system from a manual to a computer system," he said. "Since you have the list with the lowest part numbers, we're going to test run the change on your records. You continue to do things the way you are, and the new person will run the same system in parallel using the computer."

"You don't need another person," I said. "I can do both."

"No, you can't," the supervisor said.

"Yes, I can. I can do both," I said matter-of-factly.

"All right, Jim, give it a go, but if you mess up, you'll be answering to me."

"Fair enough," I said. I took both assignments, maintained the records on both systems, and by early afternoon my work was done. I had nothing left to do.

"Jeez, Jim, it was bad enough when you were getting your job done ahead of time. Now you're doing two jobs and still finishing ahead of the rest of us. Do you know how that makes us look?" It was the same coworker. I couldn't understand it. Why didn't these people want to speed up the efficiency of the company? Why didn't they care about doing the best work possible? I couldn't figure it out at the time, but it made me uncomfortable. I didn't like feeling guilty for doing what I was able.

I worked in the office for only four months more. Then I was offered a supervisor's job in the plant. I didn't know if I got the job because the company thought I was the best choice or because some coworker with influence wanted me out of the office. It didn't matter. I finally was going to be a supervisor in the company on the shop floor. I didn't care if the company thought I was ready or not. I knew I was. I recounted all the lessons I had learned along the way. I remembered how I respected Duggan and his kindness. I remembered being held back by my supervisor on the floor and taken for granted in the job shop. I remembered the threats I had received for working too hard. I remembered the slacker talk from the workers in the office. I thought hard about these things and how they would influence my leadership style. One thing for sure, I was going to be different. I would find a way to weave Duggan's humanity into my approach and weed out the things in bosses I had come to abhor. I was inventing myself as a leader. I relished the challenge.

But when I found out the area I was going to supervise, I wondered what I had done to deserve such a punishment. I was given the worst line in the building. It was filled with the toughest, meanest union-represented workers in the plant. The chief steward worked there. So did one of the more notorious committeemen. And the son of the union secretary was on the line too. When I walked in the first day, 42 pairs of eyes that looked like steel and concrete fixed on me and then turned away as if to dismiss my very presence.

My boss explained, "The poor bastard before you failed miserably, Jim. We thought it best not to have him train you. The supervisor on the next line over will tell you what you need to know." He motioned the other line supervisor to come over.

"Hi. You must be Jim," the other supervisor said.

"Yeah, I'm the new supervisor here."

"Yeah, right, okay. See that?" he asked, pointing to the beginning of the line. I nodded. "That's the beginning of your line. Down there," he pointed again, "is the end of your line. And next to that is your other line. You're responsible for everything in between. Now if those union bastards give you any trouble you can't handle, gimme a holler. Me and the other supervisors will come and bail you out. Got it?" I nodded again. That was it. That was my introduction to management. The supervisor left, without offering any more help.

I looked over my territory. There was scrap all over the place, stacks of past-due orders, mounds of rework. The line was deplorable. What was worse was that the employees on the line hated me without even knowing me. Because I was management, I was despicable to them. No matter what kind of man I was, what my beliefs were, or what I might offer them, I was hated without reason and without contemplation. The bite of this prejudice stung me—hard. It felt like a cheap shot in a basketball game, an unseen elbow in the back under the net. I wanted to fight back, but I knew such behavior would only make things worse for me.

The first night I was on duty, a small group of employees approached me.

"We're filin' this grievance against you. You gotta answer it."

My stomach tightened. Grievance? Answer? Nobody had told me how to deal with an issue like this. I didn't even know what a grievance was.

"I'm not answerin' this thing tonight," I said, trying to exert some semblance of authority.

"Yes, you are, boss man. It's a grievance, and you gotta answer it."

"Well, I'll tell you what, I'm not answerin' anything until I check it out and understand what I'm supposed to do. So you're just gonna have to wait." I turned my back on the group, trying to disguise my fear. I heard them shuffle away, chuckling and joking among themselves. They were confident they would break me. I could hear it in their laughter.

The grievance came two weeks before the two-week summer shutdown. For those two weeks, I experienced every form of harassment imaginable. Machines were sabotaged. The men treated me with disrespect, calling me hurtful names and purposely misunderstanding my orders. Work was delayed. I was failing. The vision I held about a team of people all working together for the common good of the company, energized and excited about work, seemed like nothing more than a pipe dream. Thankfully, the shutdown came. I went home to think about whether I really wanted to spend the rest of my working career in such a foul environment.

One night during the shutdown, I went outside and sat down on the back step of my home. It was almost ten o'clock, and an infinite number of stars filled the sky. I sat for a long time looking up at the stars, trying to find an answer. As I watched the sky, I was reminded of another time when I had waited alone in the night. It wasn't that long ago when I stood in the gravel parking lot of the plant ready to face the men from the shop floor who had threatened me because I ran my equipment too fast. I remembered the feeling that had come from deep down inside of me when they hadn't shown up. I remembered the relief and exhilaration that extended from my gut to every bone and muscle in my body. I had won a great personal victory that night. The same stars that watched over me then now twinkled the same message. Stand tall, Jim. Don't give up. If you give up now, you'll never conquer your fears. Be a leader. Be strong.

As the horizon drifted from black to gray to bright morning orange and then faded to pink and blue, I knew I would stay a supervisor. But I also knew I couldn't manage those guys by fear and intimidation. I was only 27 years old. I wasn't ready to be a casualty of the war between the beliefs of the company and the union. Instead, I chose diplomacy. I would build their trust. I would gain their respect. I would try to be like Duggan. I would try to make their work lives better. I hoped that by demonstrating respect and trust for them, they would in turn do the same for me.

So I returned to the shop with a new strategy. The first day back, one of the workers came up to me.

"Hey, boss, I just scrapped some pieces. Thought you'd want to know." The sarcasm and challenge in his voice were unmistakable.

"Mistakes happen," I said tentatively. "Is there something I can do to help you avoid that in the future?"

Surprised by my response, he said, "Yeah, I need different tooling for the machine." I knew the tooling had been replaced just a few weeks ago and had been working up until now. I suspected I was being tested.

"Okay, well, if you think different tooling will fix the problem, I'll get it for you." And I did.

The scene was repeated dozens of times over the next several weeks. I got them everything they needed. At the same time, I didn't waiver on job expectations. I didn't let them off the hook for coming in late or taking too many breaks. But I stayed soft on the people issues. I heard through the grapevine that one of my employees had a daughter who wanted a piano. But the man, partially disabled, didn't have the money to buy one. I sold him my wife's piano for $25. I later found out I'd been scammed. He turned around and sold the piano for $50. Although the incident upset me, I stayed true to my course of action. I didn't confront the man, and I didn't discuss it with others. Slowly but surely, things started to turn around on my two lines. Within five months, the past-due orders completely vanished. Rework was virtually nonexistent. The lines had gone from the lowest performers to among the highest.

During this time, I heard that another employee, Everett, was on leave because he was "drying out," or recovering as an alcoholic. I decided to visit him in the hospital and encourage him to get well and come back to work. Hospital rules said I had to be locked in the room with Everett and couldn't leave without permission.

"You know, Everett," I said as we sat together waiting for the door to be unlocked, "you do pretty darn good work. The line isn't the same when you're not there. And the other guys miss you too."

"Really?" Everett said without commitment.

"Yeah, you know, you got such a great sense of humor too. Man, the place isn't the same without your stories and jokes. You know when you're gone, work just isn't as much fun," I said.

"You mean it?" Everett asked.

"Yeah, Everett, I do. I hope you get better real soon. I want you back on the line. So do your buddies."

I could see tears welling up in Everett's eyes. The click of the door unlocking allowed me a graceful exit and gave Everett time to regain his composure. As I left, I called back, "See ya soon, buddy. Get well, we're all rootin' for ya."

The men on the lines couldn't fathom what I was up to. Nobody ever went to see someone when they were "taking the cure." Somehow, though, my employees respected what I did. And when Everett came back, the first thing he did was ask me how many pieces I wanted him to run.

"Everett, I want you to do as much as you can. We're both being paid pretty well by the company. I think we all should give as much effort as we can. Run as much as you can as long as you run it well," I said. In those days, most people ran less than 100 percent. From then on, Everett ran his machine consistently at 125 percent. Of course, it might have been more, because the system could only acknowledge 125 percent production. But I knew Everett was running the machine at the highest level he could.

The efficiency of the line was testament to the impact of my new approach and style of leadership. But there was one employee, the son of the union secretary, who just never produced more than 85 percent. It didn't matter how I treated him. It didn't matter whether I encouraged him. It didn't matter if I challenged him to show what he had. He simply stayed at 85 percent, no more, no less. Then, one night, the plant superintendent caught me by the arm. "Hey, you need to talk to your problem child," he said.

"Why?" I asked.

"Well, I was walking the line and saw him with an earphone on. He has a portable radio attached to his ear."

"All right, I'll go tell him to put it away," I said. Listening to the radio at work was forbidden. The company required employees to concentrate on their jobs and the machinery they operated. Radios could be distracting and could mask warning sounds made by a machine about to go awry. And they could be a safety problem. I dreaded this discussion, but the rules were clear and made sense.

"Stuart, I hear you been listening to the radio while operating the machines. You know that's a safety hazard. How 'bout puttin' it away and takin' it home?"

"Too late," Stuart said sardonically. "Joe was already down here. He ripped me a new one. Chewed me out. Threatened to fire me if he ever saw me within a foot of a radio."

"He did what?" I asked in disbelief.

"Well, he kicked my ass. He yelled at me. He called me every name in the book."

I could feel my blood pressure rising. I turned and started to walk away from Stuart's machines.

"Where ya goin', Jim?" Stuart asked.

"To see Joe."

I could feel my anger mounting as I marched deliberately toward the superintendent's office. On the way, I ran into my own general foreman—my immediate supervisor.

"Jeez, Jim, what's up with you?" he asked, sensing my ire. "Where you off to in such a huff?"

"To Joe's office," I said curtly.

"What for?" my supervisor asked.

"That's between Joe and me," I barked. I wasn't going to let anyone dissuade me from my mission. I reached Joe's office, banged on the door, and went in before Joe beckoned me.

"Why do I have this?" I said, pointing to a small blue and gold shield attached to my shirt pocket. The shield identified me as a supervisor. "Why do I have this?" I asked again. Joe was dumbfounded. I ripped the shield off my shirt and tossed it on Joe's desk. Joe looked confused.

"I don't need this and you don't need me if you're going to supervise my people. I quit," I said. With that, I turned and walked out of the office.

"Wait a minute, Jim, hold on," Joe said calmly, trying to diffuse the situation. But I just kept on walking. I walked down the hall and past the shop floor. The guys could see me heading out, with Joe trailing me. They could hear Joe imploring me to stop from time to time, but I just kept on walking—past the shop, past the time clock, out the door, into the parking lot.

Finally, Joe caught up with me in the parking lot. "Jim, Jim, no need to get so upset. I was just trying to help you enforce a little discipline, that's all," he said.

"That's my job," I said defiantly. "If you want to manage my people, go ahead. You don't need me and you don't need my ideas. If you want to interfere with what I've got going, fine. You don't need me."

"Shit, Jim, we need you. Look, if I promise to stay out of your hair and let you take care of things, will you come back?"

"I'll come back if you let me handle my people. You got a problem with them, the problem comes to me and I'll handle it. That's my job, not yours."

"Okay, Jim, I won't ever do that kind of thing if you come back."

"Done," I said. Joe extended his hand and I shook it. I accepted his apology, but I wanted him to know this was serious stuff. There was no backslapping or management camaraderie over this incident. I wanted Joe to stay out of my way. I needed him to understand that although I was forgiving him this infraction, a repeat of the incident would be totally unacceptable.

Word of the incident spread through the lines like wildfire. The story was retold in unbelieving whispers. The employees didn't want to give too much credit to a management guy, but they were in awe. I went to bat for them, offered up my job in their defense. No one had ever done that before.

As I came back onto the lines, I didn't notice any change. But the next morning when I looked at the production sheets, Stuart had run 100 percent.

* * *

My success with the renegade line spread throughout the plant. Old-time managers and rookies talked among themselves like kids who had just seen a magician. "How'd he do that?" they wondered. "What tricks does he have that we don't know about?" Like children in the audience, they were amazed at what my "magic" produced. The worst line in the plant running at the highest productivity and efficiency was nothing short of astonishing. While the higher-ups couldn't figure out exactly how I did what I did, they were keenly aware of my significant accomplishment. I was noticed by the people who counted, and although I didn't know it at the time, I had earned something every ambitious person craves—credibility. Credibility among the gatekeepers of power and position was the key I needed to unlock my future. Over time, I would recognize how potent credibility was in advancing in the company. But at this point, I was just happy to know I was on my way. I gratefully accepted the accolades heaped upon me, not knowing how addictive approval and praise would become.

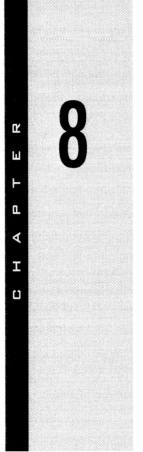

8

THE LINE
ON FIRE

Knowledge may give weight,
but accomplishments give luster.

—LORD CHESTERFIELD*

Μy credibility with management bolstered my confidence and opened up more and more opportunities. I became a roving foreman at the plant, filling in for other foremen when they were absent or on vacation. I liked the variety and the new experiences of working with different people. As I circulated through the plant, I found I was developing a reputation as a "can-do" sort of leader. This newfound respect and admiration had a strange and subtle effect on me. I began to feel "bigger," and with this bigness came a nebulous feeling of power. This feeling fueled new actions for me. I began to "take on" some of the management people who had irritated and intimidated me

---

*Permission granted from *The Forbes Book of Business Quotations,* Ted Goodman, editor, Black Dog and Leventhal Publishers, 1997, New York, NY.

in the past. I emulated the tone and word choice of the managers I had heard before. I was tougher, meaner, and more aggressive in dealing with complaints and accusations. I gradually became aware of my physical stature. I was a big man, and when I stood tall and tough, my appearance became a giant billboard of the power I now wielded. I used gruff and blustering words to let people know who was boss. At first, I was surprised at how people cowered and cringed with my toughness. But, after a while, I grew to expect that response.

In spite of my success with this approach, inside my gut I felt something wasn't exactly right. My new management style, although effective, seemed out of kilter with the way I had achieved success with the employees on the worst lines. Yet no matter where I looked, I found the most successful managers were tough birds who allowed no dissention in the ranks. This observation caused me significant anxiety. Had I just been lucky with the line? Was it a fluke that my personal attention and advocacy for the group made them achieve more? Would my efforts with the line erode over time as the workers figured out they could take advantage of me? These doubts nipped at my newfound confidence. I looked around at my peers and knew that the management style I had used with the worst line in the plant was not shared among the supervisors.

"I must have been damn lucky to be successful with that group," I thought to myself. "I might not be so lucky next time." So I watched and learned what the most successful managers did and copied those traits into my own style as best I could.

My success allowed me to progress quickly through the ranks of supervision. My natural competitiveness and ability to learn from those around me further propelled my knowledge and capability. On one assignment, I was asked to supervise a third-shift line that was significantly past due on deadlines and on the brink of shutting down the whole assembly line. As things cleared after the shift change the first night, Jesse, a senior hourly employee, came to me and said, "If you will listen to me, I will tell you how to manage the line."

I answered, "I'm listening."

Jesse told me employee by employee which person should be doing which job. He explained who had what skills and how those skills fit with each part of the manufacturing process. I listened closely and followed Jesse's recommendations. His advice turned out to be absolutely correct. Because of his years in the plant, Jesse had knowledge and experience that were invaluable in making the line run smoothly. I thanked Jesse for his help and wrote a commendation for placement in his personnel record.

By the end of the first week, the bottleneck had vanished. Parts started flowing consistently through the line to the assembly area. Before the regular supervisor had left on vacation, he had scheduled Sunday overtime for the last machine in the process, anticipating a final crunch to get the work through the line. But when the operator came in that night, there was no work to do. Jesse's suggestions had so improved the workflow that the overtime wasn't needed. The company paid the operator four hours of call-in pay at double time and sent him home.

During the last days that I was filling in, I walked the line as usual. One night, I found Jesse listening to the radio—a violation of company policy and a safety hazard. I thought back to the first time I'd run into this problem, with Stuart in the shop. "Why do we have to have radios?" I thought to myself, slightly annoyed. "They always end up causing me trouble!" But in this case, I recognized how much Jesse had helped me. He had been the catalyst for an incredible turnaround in a very short time. I knew that without Jesse's help, I still would be struggling with the assignment. So on the spur of the moment, I decided to walk away without saying anything. I was so indebted to Jesse for his help. But after a few steps, I realized that if I ignored this infraction, I would be selling out not just my credibility as a supervisor but my own integrity.

"Jesse, you know the rules," I said gently, but firmly. "Please take the radio out of your ear and put it in your toolbox until the morning, and then take it home."

"You son-of-a-bitch," Jesse yelled. "I was listening to a replay of the Bradley basketball game. I save your management ass the last couple of weeks, and you won't even let me listen to a basketball game. That's the last time I help anyone like you!"

I held Jesse's gaze. "Jesse, it's wrong. It's against the rules. I'm asking you to respect our rules."

Jesse was furious when I turned to walk away. As I thought about the confrontation, I turned back and faced him. "Jesse, in just two weeks I have gained more respect for you than any employee I've had the privilege to work with in my life. How could you possibly respect me as a supervisor if I walked by something like this without dealing with it?"

Jesse stared at me for a long time. Finally, he dropped his eyes, put his hand out, and said quietly, "You're right, Jim." Years into the future, whenever I returned to Peoria, I would make it a point to go back to the line and spend some time with Jesse. No matter what, he always took a few moments to talk with me. I learned two important lessons that night—be steady and true with your convictions and be consistent in your treatment of all people, regardless of what favors you might owe them.

Soon, I was asked to interview for a position as a general foreman under one of the meanest, toughest superintendents in the company. Howard was known for screaming at workers and could unleash a string of profanities without batting an eye. He was fearless with his invectives. He once was placed on suspension for six months for calling a vice president "stupid." But he had to be good; otherwise, he would have been fired for that remark and many other fits of rage. I personally had never experienced Howard's ire, but I had witnessed it enough to imagine the pain it could inflict. Nonetheless, the job was a great opportunity for me to move ahead in the company, so I agreed to the interview.

"Jim," Howard said, "You know you're pretty damn lucky to get this interview. No one as young as you has ever been considered to be a general foreman on first shift."

"Yes, sir, I know," I answered respectfully.

"Well, do you think you're up to it? I do. I've seen how you handle yourself with the guys, I've seen..."

Howard's sentence was interrupted by a meek "Excuse me..." from the doorway. It was the man I was supposed to replace as general foreman.

"What the hell do you want, you son of a bitch?" Howard bellowed.

I didn't hear the answer. My mind was racing. "Is this the kind of man I want to work for? Do I want to be treated like this? Can I take this kind of abuse?" I thought of some of the lessons I'd learned. Don't break the rules. Work hard. Be consistent. Maintain your integrity. "If I can just do all these things, I think I can be okay," I told myself. "As long as I don't piss him off, he'll leave me alone, I'm sure."

I took the job, keeping the rules I had learned over the years in mind. Again I went into an area tense with antagonism. The nine supervisors reporting to me were experienced—some of them old enough to be my father—and they resented my youth and inexperience. The hourly people wondered whose apple I'd polished to get such a prime position. But I didn't care. I used the same techniques I had applied in my first supervisory job. I got people the things they needed. I helped out where I could. I provided coaching and annual performance reviews—it was hard to believe some of the supervisors hadn't had performance reviews for years. As a result, the group started working together. The tension eased. Production went up, way up.

One day, Howard caught me by the arm, "Hey, Jim, do you know what I did for you today?" I had no idea. I couldn't tell if this would be good news or bad.

"What?" I asked.

"I put in for a raise for you. They turned me down this time, Jim, because you haven't been here long enough. But I'm going to keep turnin' it in until you get that raise."

"That's great, Howard. I appreciate it." The harsh man's vote of confidence buoyed me. It was like getting an "A" from the hardest teacher in school or being recruited by Vince Lombardi. The attention from a man so hard to please made me want to work even harder.

***

It was the mid-1960s, and the company was growing and expanding into a global market. Demand was high, and the plants were stressed to meet deadlines. Slowing down production could mean a missed deadline. And a missed deadline was the greatest infraction a plant could make.

It was one of those days when production schedules seemed absolutely impossible. The engineering work on the tractors during a product update was troublesome. The tractors wouldn't run and couldn't be driven, so they were dragged off the assembly line with a giant overhead crane. The stress of the mammoth tractors on the crane caused it to heat up. My team and I had to watch the crane to make sure it didn't break down under its heavy workload.

This day, there were many tractors to be taken off the assembly line. There were inoperable tractors sitting everywhere. I knew that a production shortfall would have dire consequences—as dire as the time I ran scrap in the apprentice program. One thing was sure, I was not going to make the same mistake twice. I would not embarrass my superintendent with a loss of production. I would not break the rules.

I kept the overhead crane running at a higher than normal pace. Soon the burden of the overload could be detected with the rancid smell of something electrical burning. Thin blue smoke started to waft off the overhead crane.

"Let's shut her down," the operator told me.

"Hell no," I responded. "Keep her goin', we've gotta make the schedule."

"But boss, it looks like she's catchin' fire," the operator pleaded.

"I don't care. Keep her running," I yelled.

Soon small flames erupted from the crane.

"Shut her down now?" the operator demanded.

"No, sir, we keep her going." And with that, I enlisted some workers to help pull the heavy equipment along the crane rail, making sure the assembly line didn't miss a beat.

"Hey, shut her down and shut her down now," a union committeeman said to me.

"I ain't shuttin' her down," I said firmly.

"Then I'm going to Howard. You can't do this. It ain't right. You're gonna set the whole place on fire."

"Do what you have to, but we're not missing this deadline," I yelled back. We continued to push and pull equipment down the rail. The crane continued to smoke and sputter and flame.

All of a sudden, there was an eerie silence in the shop. I looked over my shoulder and saw Howard coming. His shirtsleeves were rolled up mid-arm, like he was getting ready for a fight. A pipe hung tensely from his mouth, and smoke was coming out of it like an old locomotive climbing a steep hill. All the employees in the area watched my movements—I could feel the eyes of the workers in the shop fixed on me. I knew they were waiting for Howard to unload on me. I knew they were waiting for him to give me a tongue-lashing I'd never forget. The workforce was anxious and tense.

But I kept dragging the machines off the assembly line. Finally, Howard walked up to me and said in a very low voice so no one else would hear, "You think you can keep this son of a bitch running until the end of the shift, Jimbo?" he asked.

I said, "Don't worry. We'll keep it running."

Howard chuckled to himself. I sensed he knew the overhead crane posed no real, immediate danger to employees and that its physical appearance was more of an agitation than anything else. "Jim, you're a chip off the old block," he said as he turned and went back to his office.

***

The lesson was clear to everyone there. Make the company look good. Make the deadlines. Make the money. No matter what it takes. No matter how hard. No matter what the risk. Please the boss, please the company. And when you please the boss, you are generously rewarded. My toughness and determination not only got the job done for the company, but also made me a hero with the most unyielding man in the plant. The pride and sense of accomplishment I felt that day were indescribable. As I watched the smoldering crane, I vowed I would keep my own internal fire going, that I would never cease to seek this sense of triumph. I would learn and perfect the attitudes and skills I needed to feed my hunger for the feeling of success I had that day. Sweaty and tired and smelling of smoke, I basked in my achievement. No, I wasn't thinking about the people I might have hurt. I was thinking about me.

THIEVES
IN THE NIGHT

Unless you enter the tiger's den,
you cannot take the cubs.

—JAPANESE PROVERB

In 1965, while the nation was beginning to deal with the challenges of the civil rights movement and the Vietnam War, the company was surging ahead. It was just coming off a year with a two-for-one stock split. More than 50,000 people worked for the earthmoving giant. Profits soared by more than 20 percent over the previous year. Across the country—no, the world—the company's distinctive yellow machinery was working. And if the market in one global area diminished, like magic, a new market appeared. The company began equipment production in Japan with one of that country's industrial giants. Bigger, better engines entered the product line. The company's world headquarters was under construction in a small midwestern city previously know for Vaudeville, vice, and Fibber Magee and Molly.

In the midst of all this, the earthmoving colossus acquired a small, family-owned enterprise in one of the more questionable parts of Cleveland. Known for its forklift trucks, this new division of Caterpillar was expected to bring yet another strong product into the company's ever-expanding line of high-quality equipment. The little forklift enterprise had grown up in a neighborhood that had withered with time. Small bungalows and townhouses once inhabited by middle-class folks were abandoned as those who were able fled to the suburbs. Now, people faded with poverty lived near the plant. With poverty came its unfortunate cousins—crime, decay, despair. The people of the plant and the surrounding area had become tough and unforgiving to survive in such a place. But the company wasn't worried. Its will was strong. Its leaders were powerful. Like the scrapers and excavators and dozers it built, the company was confident its employees could change the landscape of the rough enterprise. Under the strict guidance of the giant company, the Ohio plant would perform and succeed.

By now I had molded myself into a hardened company man. Under the tutelage of the tough old cowboy Howard, I had harnessed a rugged sense of power. Employees respected me. I could feel it. They did what I asked them to, and they liked it. My success was cyclical—each success just led to another. My reputation grew, and with it grew my sense of myself.

Howard helped reinforce my changing demeanor. The boss man treated me as a son. Gloria and I became regular dinner guests at Howard's home following his retirement. He often praised me as a man who could deal with the rough-and-tumble union workers. He constantly found ways to recognize and reinforce me. He wanted me to know how much he valued me. In an unconventional and unprecedented move, Howard shared a part of himself with me that he had shared with no one else beyond family—at least not without a price. On several occasions when Gloria and I were guests, Howard took me to his basement and, from special safes, he pulled out magnificent gold and silver coins from his long-held collection. Many of these treasures he gave to me. I was confused and embarrassed at first by this generosity. But he persisted. As time passed, each coin laid gently in my hand by Howard became symbolic of my achievement and Howard's appreciation for my loyalty.

Later, I was invited by the factory manager to play golf at a local country club as a reward for shipping products on schedule for the U.S. military. As our foursome approached the 18th green to finish the round, I saw a man standing on the green in a suit and tie. As we got closer, I recognized the man as Howard.

"What the hell are you doing out here?" I asked.

"Jim, I didn't know you enjoyed golf," Howard said. "And when I found out, I decided to buy you something."

Embarrassed, I asked, "What did you buy?"

"I bought you a membership in this club."

"Howard, I can't accept this," I answered.

"Of course you can. Why wouldn't you?"

"I wouldn't accept it anyway, Howard, but I've just been offered an assignment in Cleveland. I'll be moving out of the area. No one knows this yet, so let's keep it between you and me," I explained.

Howard's expression was mixed, proud that I had been chosen, but sad to see me move on. He put his arm around me and said, "That's great, Jim. I've had a hell of a good time working with you. I'm damn proud of you."

I thanked Howard for his generosity and the lessons of leadership he had taught me.

"You know, Howard," I said. "I've been told I'm the only person you never raised your voice in anger to. That means a lot to me."

Howard smiled. "There's a reason why I didn't. You understand what it was," he said. "I'm going to miss you." Then he turned and walked off the green. That was the last time I ever saw him. Less than a year later, Howard died suddenly from a heart attack.

***

Although Cleveland was hours away from home, it had much of the same midwestern feel to it as Peoria. I found the adjustment to the community much easier to make than our family's first move from rural Greenview to the city of Peoria. But

I was not prepared for what I saw at the newly acquired facility. Caterpillar's professional standards were clearly not yet evident. The plant was led by friends of the former owners who viewed themselves more as aristocracy than as managers and had let the environment deteriorate into a war zone. The "serfs" of the union looked for any way they could to unburden themselves of the autocratic control of their leaders. The leaders in turn rebuffed these challenges with the disinterested harshness of King Louis XIV and his wife, Marie Antoinette. At Christmas time, for example, the docks were loaded with outrageous presents for the aristocratic managers—shotguns, freezers filled with beef, pianos, and other expensive merchandise. The managers accepted these gifts as tributes from their suppliers. After all, without the *noblesse oblige* of the company leaders, where would the vendors sell their wares? The underlings of the company witnessed the extravagances with jealousy and anger. The homage paid to uncaring leaders made their oppression more suffocating. Because of this hand of unequal leadership, the plant became constantly confrontational. Like the soldiers of the French Revolution, the line workers engaged in relentless skirmishes with authority, trying to loosen the reign of terror and regain their sense of dignity as human beings.

I had no idea what I was walking into. I expected the Cleveland union people to share the same aggressive, antagonistic demeanor as those I had already encountered. I wasn't worried. My skill and position had helped tame that demeanor in East Peoria. I had no reason to believe that I would not be able to use my sense of persuasion with the Cleveland group.

When I first got to the plant, I did what any good manager would do. I checked the performance of the organization. I was astounded to find that most of the orders were way overdue for shipment to customers. In fact, many of the orders were at least a *year past due*. I couldn't believe it. As I met the leaders of the small company, I found they harbored a strong resentment of new management. They had done just fine without the big company's influence—thank you very much—and they would continue to be fine without them. But worse than their attitudes toward the new owners was their lack of teamwork. No one could agree on anything except that whatever was wrong with the company, it was someone else's fault.

As our new group tried to calm the explosive situation, things just got worse. As outsiders, we brought a new pressure to the company. The plant began to explode into small wildcat strikes. These strikes perplexed me. I didn't see the sense in them. Nothing was ever resolved, really. But the strikes seemed to act like a pressure valve. When things got too hot in the plant, it would release its tension with one of these strikes. The workers felt a temporary relief from the oppression of their bosses. They, not their managers, had control during these strikes. In an organization built on fear and intimidation, this release seemed to be as natural as the changing of the seasons. What neither group seemed to realize, however, was that with the release of this pressure came the loss of steam that allowed the company to move and speed ahead. But no one seemed to care much about the company's success. They seemed only to focus on what they wanted and what they didn't have.

The rest of the managers and I respected the strikes as best we could. We didn't work the lines. We didn't try to make production schedules. But as managers, we were expected to show up at work, break through the picket lines, put in an honest day's work, and demonstrate the unwavering will of the company. We were expected to safeguard those who did decide to cross the lines to perform their jobs. We were expected to stand firm, maintaining order. But never, never were we expected or permitted to do the work of the union people on the line. To make sure of this, senior managers like me often patrolled the shop at night, looking for whoever might be there.

One night as I walked my patrol in the dim glow of the safety light of the shop, I felt as if I were being watched or followed. My eyes darted left and right, then over my shoulder. Nothing. My stomach tightened, and my mouth became dry and salty. As I turned my head, a figure stepped out from the shadows of a pillar. I saw a gleam of silver, then felt a sinister coldness against my forehead. Without thinking, I ripped the steel away from my face. In my hand I found a .38 pistol. Loaded.

When I looked up to see who was threatening me, I was surprised to see the face of an hourly worker I knew well.

"Dick, what are you thinkin'?" I asked. "You're not a killer. You're not like this. What happened to you?"

Dick said nothing.

"Here, take this damned thing home, Dick." I handed the loaded weapon back. "Don't ever bring it back inside the company again. Go home, Dick, just go home."

The man looked up, startled.

"You ain't firin' me?" he asked.

"No, Dick, not this time, because I know this isn't you. But I don't want to see that thing anywhere near here again," I replied.

"Okay, boss, okay." Dick slipped the .38 into his pocket, turned, and quickly walked to the exit.

"I could have been killed," I thought. "But I wasn't, I wasn't." Without real notice, my confidence grew, and somewhere deep inside me I knew I was becoming one tough bastard. My power and influence were further confirmed the next time I saw Dick and the time after and the time after. Not only was he a human reminder of my courage, but in his gratitude he had become an informant, a fink who kept me up-to-date on every malicious move of the union.

After a while, the strikes became part of the expected routine. Things would settle down, then heat up, then the strike would come. The workers expressed their frustrations with threats—some they followed through on, but most were just trash talk. Like trauma doctors who come to accept horror in their jobs and deal with it in an orderly, routine manner, management became desensitized to the strikes. We knew what to do, when, and how. We anticipated the confrontations and encounters. Each of these strikes eroded the humanity of the people involved. The threats made, the verbal abuse, the shaking fists, the angry eyes dehumanized those who used them. It was easy after a while to look at the faces contorted with rage as irrational humans. And the only way to deal with unreasonable people is with sheer force. So it went. I got used to this rhythm of the organization. I developed my own strengths to navigate this brutal world of work. Living with fear of physical harm became as much a part of my routine as parting my hair.

During one of the strikes, six large articulated forklift trucks were due for delivery. They were unusual pieces of equipment, unique to the industry, that could not be purchased from other suppliers. They were designed to work in narrow aisles. The company that ordered them absolutely needed them by the contracted date for a huge grand opening of a new warehouse. To assure delivery, the company had negotiated a severe financial penalty for every day late. Unfortunately, the purchase agreement made no allowance for a strike. I recognized the situation as something I had learned at an early age. Break the rules, pay the price. In this case, the price was hundreds of dollars for each day of delay. The plant manager called me into his office.

"Jim, we've got to ship those forklifts. If we don't, we're all in deep trouble."

"What? Are you serious? We'll get killed if we go anywhere near those shipping docks," I said.

"They've got to ship, Jim."

"Those guys are armed with guns, bats, crowbars, grenades…you name it. It ain't safe."

"I don't care, Jim. They have to ship."

"How do you expect us to do that?" I asked.

"Don't care, Jim. Just get it done."

I opened my mouth to plead with the boss. Before I could speak, he cut me off. "No argument, Jim. Just get it done. Now get the hell out of my office."

I spent the next couple of days trying to figure out how to ship the forklifts. Diplomacy wouldn't work. If the strikers knew how important the shipment was, they would never let up. In fact, they'd make matters worse. I knew I couldn't depend on the union for understanding. In fact, I couldn't depend on any union to help in any way whatsoever. The Teamsters, who would be needed to drive the rigs to deliver the products, would stand behind the striking laborers as well. I realized if we managed to ship the forklifts, it would be one of the most embarrassing and demoralizing blows to the union ever. If we got caught, there was no escape. I had never fought in a war for my country, but with this assignment, I knew I had become a soldier of the company. So I decided to "steal" the forklifts.

I enlisted the help of two daring supervisors—tough guys, fearless men. As I explained the challenge, the men realized the risk and difficulty of pulling it off. We worked on our plan like generals planning the invasion of Normandy. Conditions had to be right. Timing had to be perfect. Stealth and surprise were paramount. No mistakes, no mistakes, or the consequences would be severe.

The three of us convinced a nonunion trucking company to participate in the plan—for a very high premium, of course.

The plant was a large, rectangular building located on a corner and at the bottom of a hill on 152nd Street. On the south side was the employee entrance. The front door, plant offices, and gate to the shipping dock all were located around the corner on the east side of the building.

For several nights, we watched the rhythm of the picket line. The line did not patrol the south and east sides at the same time. Instead, the picketers walked the entire south side, turned left, and then walked the entire east side. Next, they would turn and follow the same path back to the far west corner of the south side. The building was a huge structure. It took the picketers several minutes to walk the distance of the south side, turn, and then walk back. We realized there was enough time to get the on-highway trucks inside plant property to the docks without being seen or heard.

We rehearsed the plan in our minds over and over again. Finally, we were ready. Late one night, the on-highway trucks perched at the top of the hill—lights out, motors silent. We sat in my car, watching in the shadows for the pickets to take their southern walk. The time came. I started the engine, put the car into gear, and rolled to the east side entrance. One of the other supervisors jumped out, quietly unlocked the gate, and I drove through. The gate closed behind us.

I drove the car, lights out, down the backside of the building and parked in the shadows. I walked back to the gate to watch the picketers. When they were out of sight, I flashed the lights three times. The on-highway trucks silently rolled down the hill, through the gate to the docks. When both trucks were inside, the gate was locked. As the picketers returned to the front of the building, we were already hidden in darkness behind the building.

Now we waited. We would not move again until the picket line moved to the south side. This stop-and-start activity reminded me of scenes I had seen in a movie—*Stalag 17*. The prisoners could only escape outside the glare of the strong searchlights. But instead of one bright light scrutinizing the area, we faced detection by dozens of pairs of eyes. I secretly wondered which was worse—a bright searchlight like they had to dodge in the stalag or the hateful stares of the union workers' eyes. Ultimately, it didn't matter. Be caught in either and your life was in peril.

When the picketers were away, we opened the doors on the dock. There the special forklift trucks stood silent, eerie shadows in a dim room lit only by the yellow glow of an aisle safety light. We reached for the crowbars. We would not drive the forklifts onto the on-highway trucks. We were too close to the picketers on the south side, and the sound of engines starting would give us away. So each of us took a crowbar, wedged it under a back tire, and put our shoulders into it. The tie bar pinched the tire forward. Slowly, carefully, silently, we inched the forklifts forward from the factory to the dock onto the trucks.

I noticed something strange as I worked. I couldn't say I wasn't afraid—I was. But my fear was something that drove me onward, drove me toward success. In my mind's eye, I could picture the anxiety a successful mission would create for the union. I could see how this would be an incredible blow for them. I reveled in the thought that they would have to admit a kind of defeat. They would be outmaneuvered—by management. This picture was so strong and powerful that I coveted it with all my life. There was no way I would fail.

Push and pinch. Push and pinch. The forklifts edged onto the waiting on-highway trucks. The first one was loaded. Five to go. Push and pinch. Now wait. The picketers are coming. Hold your breath. Don't sneeze. Don't cough. You are soldiers of the company. Complete your mission. Quiet now. The picketers' steps are fading. Strain your ears. Anyone around? No. Good. Go again. Push and pinch. Push and pinch.

The routine went on until six forklifts were loaded and the doors were quietly shut. All attention now was focused on the picketers. When they were farthest away from the docks, the on-highway trucks started their engines and groaned up the hill and out of the plant onto 152nd Street. There, they turned left to avoid detection.

Once they were over the hill, the trucks stopped along the road and waited for me and the two other supervisors. When we were reassembled, the caravan drove several blocks, then parked along the street. We got into the trucks again and nailed wedges in front and behind the forklifts' wheels to hold them in position during the journey. Once this was done, the trucks left to deliver the products to the customer.

During the remainder of the strike, no mention was made by anyone about the disappearance of the forklifts. The plant manager, however, was obviously pleased. "There was no question in my mind, Jim, that you would get it done." I knew exactly what "it" was. I remembered how exuberant I felt as the trucks rumbled up the hill and onto 152nd Street. I remembered the sweet taste of victory as I watched the tail lights of those trucks fade in the distance, carrying the company cargo "stolen" from behind "enemy lines." But the manager's comment, succinct as it was, made me feel like I had been awarded a special decoration or medal for going above and beyond the call of duty, for distinguished service, for uncommon valor. I savored this feeling throughout the remainder of the strike.

* * *

Months later, when the strike was over, the union president approached me. "There were six forklifts shipped during the strike," he said. "I don't know how it was done. I don't know how it could have been done, but I do know you must have had something to do with it." I said nothing. I didn't blink. I walked away. The feeling of victory and accomplishment that I had savored through the strike was even more amplified by the deference of the union president. My emotions were unbelievable. For the first time, I experienced the heady sense of triumph the victor feels as he looks back toward the vanquished. Indeed, for a small moment I was the company's conquering hero. I felt pride and redemption that our side had won.

Today, I remember this "glorious" incident with sadness. I see "our side" and "their side" references as grim reminders of an unproductive period. Yes, it was a conflict, a hideous internal conflict. Only when it ended, years later, did we reach our full potential.

10

THE SOUND
OF SILENCE

'Tis easier to know how to speak
than how to be silent.

—THOMAS FULLER

As time wore on for me as a manager, I found the confrontations and challenges made by the workforce only seemed to make me stronger. One time I was followed on a highway going home from work by a car full of strangers. I watched them intently in my rearview mirror, trying to lose them in traffic. When I could not, I found myself annoyed, not intimidated. It was late at night, with very little traffic, so I stopped my car in the middle of the highway, got out, and walked back to the strangers' car. "You want a piece of me?" I yelled. Immediately, they drove their car around mine, never laying a single finger on me. Then there was the time I attended the funeral of one of my African-American workers' mothers. The church was in an area of town where outsiders were not welcome. I walked into the church to pay my respects and found it packed—and there was not a single other white face among the people. Suddenly, the entire congregation went quiet. I walked down the aisle, expressed my condolences to the employee and his family, and walked back out. Safe and unmolested, I made my way home. As I climbed into bed that night, I realized how lucky I was to have been able to do this without harm. Interestingly, I had asked several others in the company to accompany me, and all had refused.

In my heart I appreciated the human spirit and cared about people, all people. But I was often afraid to show my compassionate side. I thought those I reported to would view it as a sign of weakness. They used their management positions to subjugate people, to make them bend to the will of the company. So when I was under pressure to produce and to achieve, I modeled their ways. No one told me to do this. My learning was indirect, reinforced by my superiors and my success. I was management, dammit, and determined that everyone around me knew who was boss. I was becoming like those who led me.

As the 1960s clipped violently into the 1970s, I was astounded by the absurdity of what was happening in the government, on college campuses, and in the country. Instead of firm leaders keeping the country and the student protestors in check, wishy-washy academics, soft politicians, and feel-good psychologists seemed to be undermining the very order of things. By this time, I had forgotten the feeling of oppression I had experienced when I worked for Big Stan, the man who would never promote me. I'd mentally shelved Duggan's kindness as an anomaly of management. Even though I was uncomfortable at times in a "tough guy" role, I believed others expected me to lead this way. And, after all was said and done, did I not achieve remarkable results?

In the early 1970s, my view of myself was reaffirmed. The company selected me to work with its joint venture in Japan. I realized the significance of this appointment. At age 37 I was one of the youngest men ever asked to take such a position. Even more significant was that overseas work was usually reserved for the best and brightest of the college boys. I had never received a college degree, and yet I was among the chosen few. My position, power, and ability could not have been reinforced more by the company. I knew it, and I was proud of it.

After the move to Ohio, my family and I were beginning to forget our roots to small-town Greenview. The move to Japan was just another adventure for us. We took up residence in a high-rise apartment building, located in the midst of Japanese tradition and international ambition. One block away was Prince Akihito's palace, and the Canadian Embassy was located just behind our home. We often ate at the close-by Tokyo-American Club. Predictably, the Russian Embassy faced the Club. From this vantage, the Russians were suspected of monitoring the hundreds of patrons of one of the world's largest social organizations. From the balcony window of our apartment, when the smog and clouds cleared, we could see the top of Mount Fuji. Within this decidedly Japanese world mixed with cosmopolitan interests, we made our home.

I enjoyed the cuisine of Japan. I was not afraid to eat raw fish, bird brain, a small eel delicacy called *dojo,* whole sparrow, raw chicken, and raw eggs. On less adventurous days, I would grab some sushi at a little shop across from the apartment. I was amazed at the integrity and discipline of the Japanese— there was virtually no crime. Once I left a camera on a fence post in the middle of a large park. Five hours later I returned to the park to find the camera unmoved.

Because of my position in the company, I had a driver and a car to use to and from work. None of the Americans at the plant drove to work. Most of the others went by special bus. As I became acclimated to Japan, I discovered the country had a powerful sense of social order. The Japanese language itself forced a person to make a decision to speak to another either as a superior or a subordinate. There seemed to be no allowance for peers. Respect was genuine and expected among different social and age groups. Aside from the natural pecking order of Japanese society, my size and features further distinguished me among the populace. My six-foot-four frame automatically set me apart from other men. And my wife, at five-foot-nine, towered over Japanese women. But the blonde hair of our second son drew the most attention. As we strolled through the busy streets of Tokyo, the Japanese often reached out to touch my son's hair.

The distinction of being an American in Tokyo who worked for a joint venture between two of the world's greatest industrial giants—and the trappings that accompanied this position—were not lost on me. I no longer was a farm rube, but an international businessman, a reasonably heavy-hitter, someone who could not be taken lightly. I savored this new role and craved even more from the company and the world. I had started to learn the Japanese language in Ohio before leaving. In doing so, I was reminded of how my own English was still homespun. This would not do for a man of the world who rubbed elbows with the elite internationals at the Tokyo-American Club and the Yokohama Country Club. So I hired a teacher from the international high school to perfect and sharpen my English speech and writing skills. The young man worked with me in the evenings. Sometimes I would recite what had happened during the day; other times I would put it down in writing. Then the teacher would simplify and strengthen my stories, adding structure and sophistication to my speech and writing patterns. We also worked on vocabulary. For the first time in my life, I was freeing myself of the down-home diction that separated me from others in my position. The last evidence of my difference was being erased. I truly was becoming a respectable company man.

With finely honed confidence—some might say arrogance—I was ready to create the same excitement in Japan I had at home. I had no doubt I would capture the attention of these hard-working, respectful people.

* * *

Post World War II Japan was a manufacturing disaster. Plants had been shelled, the workforce demoralized, and the quality of Japanese workmanship questioned. The small, densely populated country lacked ample land and natural resources to be self-sufficient. As a result, the Japanese understood their survival rested with their ability to import and to export to other countries. Concerned with these problems, the Union of Japanese Scientists and Engineers invited a U.S. quality control expert to their country to help them secure a dominant place in the world economy.

At first largely ignored in his own country, W. Edwards Deming, the statistical genius, brought just the right tools into the culture of Japan. Deming called for a new version of leadership where quality was measured statistically in terms of defects. He challenged management to understand the "variation" in worker performance as either a lack of training or truly a matter of diverse skills and abilities. He saw managers as helpers, people who understood the statistical implications of performance and could help individuals and the company manage fluctuations in organizational performance. Although Deming had 14 key concepts of management, the most visible at the joint-venture plant was Deming's constancy of purpose.

I recognized early on that the Japanese universally understood their need to be exceptional participants in the global economy. This recognition was a natural extension of the Japanese iron will that had won so many battles in the last World War. At the plant level, this unified purpose was expressed by the Japanese in their obsession with quality. I witnessed highly emotional interactions between workers and managers, which looked remotely like discussions I had seen in Ohio and Illinois between labor and management. The difference in Japan, however, was that workers and managers did not see each other as the adversary, but rather their outside competitors. Their animated discussions had only one outcome in mind—improving the quality of Japanese manufacturing.

I had heard that Japanese companies managed by consensus. Intellectually, I found this notion close to absurd. I'd been at the Ohio plant for years and never had management and labor been in total agreement. I was surprised, however, when I saw how the Japanese worked together. Consensus was not necessarily expected for a singular way to accomplish work. But it was expected for the outcome of work. So when groups of Japanese got together to plan strategies or solve problems, they automatically had a common sense of purpose. This constancy of purpose, as well as all the statistical tools and techniques, was a special gift from the American Deming. Other Japanese, like Kaoru Ishikawa, Noriaki Kano, and Masaaki Imai, would springboard from Deming's work to create a nation unified in its pursuit of quality.

Implicit within the Japanese order was the concept of respect. This ancient tradition complemented Deming's notion of "pride in workmanship." As part of this respect, the Japanese acknowledged the abilities and expertise of people at all levels of the plant. This respect in turn supported yet another tenet of Deming's—fear has no place in the organization. Deming realized fear was an enemy of quality improvement. Fearful workers tell the boss what he wants to hear, not what is real. Deming and the Japanese understood that without the honest observations of the front-line people who know and do the job, industrial progress was stilted at best. I observed these traits in the Japanese plant with heightened curiosity. The deference of respect was oddly balanced with a constancy of purpose that allowed—no, compelled—the Japanese, regardless of position, to participate actively in the success of the organization. This balance was foreign to me in more ways than one.

I was surprised to find that American influence was minimal at the shared plant. Each of the 21 Americans was assigned to a Japanese counterpart at the factory. In spite of this connection, I found myself restless for the first six months of my stay. I had no influence. The Japanese were polite and respectful, but I was not really included in the daily operations of the company. Neither was the rest of my American staff. The Americans, it seemed, were needed only to make the transfer of technology smoother. This limited leadership role annoyed me. As always, I wanted to be a catalyst for achievement. I wanted to have impact. But the Japanese looked at me as a benign annoyance that had to be warmly welcomed to ensure progress. I was perplexed. I shared the same insistence on accomplishment the Japanese did and was sure I could help. But the Japanese wouldn't let me into their protected world.

Although weekend trips with my family provided some diversion, I lived a professional life that bounced between irritation and boredom. The Americans reporting to me often complained about conditions at the plant. These complaints had little to do with the work, but more with the attitude of the Japanese themselves. I began keeping lists of their complaints and found mine were remarkably similar: (1) the Japanese never have time to talk to me; (2) we don't know what we are expected to do functionally; (3) we don't get invited to all meetings; (4) we don't have much to do around here; and so on. The complaints were accented by the fact that there was absolutely no trace in the plant of the American side of the joint venture. The caps and shirts of the workers were emblazoned with the logo and name of the Japanese partner, as were other reminders throughout the organization.

I found myself going stir-crazy. To keep my sanity, I often strolled through the plant. Although the workers bore little resemblance to the employees in Ohio, the product was being made in a similar way. This familiarity gave me some comfort. But as I observed the dedication of the Japanese workers and managers to principles of quality, I realized that although America contributed the product and technology, it was the Japanese and their obsession to quality and continuous improvement, to *kaizen,* that made the product better. With this realization, I felt discouragement overtaking me. I recognized I wasn't really making things happen. This absence from achievement threatened my confidence. As time wore on without an opportunity to participate in the operations of the plant, I felt depression slipping over me like the fog that sometimes drifted down the sides of Mt. Fuji toward the coast.

One day, as I sat quietly in my office reading reports over and over again to pass the time, I heard someone clear his throat. I looked up from my paperwork and saw an elderly Japanese man named Tanaka-san. Tanaka-san was part of management and had been with the company for quite some time. Wiry silver strands shimmered among his thick black crop of hair. Tanaka-san's soft face showed solemn lines of experience.

"I'm sorry," I said immediately. "I didn't see you." I wanted Tanaka-san to know I meant no disrespect by not acknowledging him. "What do you need?"

The deep brown eyes faltered in their gaze. "I need help."

"With what?" I asked.

"I am responsible for acquiring the imported material for the assembly line. There is some kind of delay stateside," Tanaka-san explained. "I cannot get what I need. I will cause the assembly line to go down."

The man didn't have to go on. I knew shutting down the line would be a great loss of face for Tanaka-san, a shame that would be difficult for him to overcome. Although I didn't realize it at the time, Tanaka-san's plea was an act of desperation.

"Okay," I said. "I'll see what I can do."

"Thank you," Tanaka-san said, bowed respectfully, and left.

I finally felt like I could contribute. I was less concerned with Tanaka-san's problem than I was excited by the possibility that I could actually *do* something for the plant. Ignoring the time difference, I called my buddies in the States. "I don't care what magic you have to perform," I demanded, "just get the iron to Japan as fast as you can."

My connections in the States came through. The iron was shipped in plenty of time. Tanaka-san did not cause the line to go down. Soon, other Japanese managers were coming to me with problems. I concluded Tanaka-san must have shared the story of his success with his peers. The sharing of problem solving with the Japanese invigorated me. I felt the fog lifting.

Tanaka-san showed up at my door one more time, much later. Happy to see him, I asked, "How can I help you, Tanaka-san?"

"I have a gift for you."

"What?" I asked.

"I have a gift for you," Tanaka-san repeated. From behind his back, he produced a small, rectangular box. I took the box carefully and opened it. Inside I found an old Japanese fan. The silk between the spines was tattered and stained. Confused, I said nothing, but looked up at Tanaka-san.

"This fan is my wife's. She used it many years ago when she was a young dancing lady. We want you to have it, Despain-san," Tanaka-san said.

"Oh, no, Tanaka-san," I said. "This has too much meaning for you and your *okusan*. I can't accept it." I felt embarrassed to receive such an intimate and priceless present. I had only done my job and to be rewarded with such a gift overwhelmed me.

"No, Despain-san, you have to take it," Tanaka-san insisted. "My *okusan* and I want you to have it."

I didn't know what to say. "Thank you, Tanaka-san, I shall treasure it." I replaced the fan carefully in the box. Tanaka-san bowed and turned to leave. At the door, Tanaka-san seemed to have forgotten something.

"Despain-san," Tanaka-san said, "I was in the war."

"Tanaka-san, that war is over and behind us. Let's not worry about it."

Tanaka-san then said, "I wanted you to know I fought the Russians, not the Americans." I reminded him again that the war was long over.

A slight smile spread across Tanaka-san's face. The solemn lines of his forehead seemed lighter and more relaxed. He bowed slightly one more time and left my office.

After that incident, I became more and more involved with the Japanese. I spent more evenings having dinner with Japanese people from the plant than I did with other Americans. I was included in meetings that previously had been off limits. I saw firsthand how management and the front line worked together. I marveled at the expansiveness of Japanese communications. The interplay between all levels in the plant proved the local saying time and time again: "There are no secrets in Japan." Yet, in spite of all the ongoing communication, the Japanese also valued silence. They used breaks in the conversation to express many feelings. Sometimes silence was used as leverage in negotiations. Sometimes it demonstrated absolute comfort with the people around—there was no need to fill empty spaces with small talk. Often it was used to show respect and recognize position in the Japanese order of things. Over a half dozen years, I came to know and like the Japanese and their culture.

A year before my family and I were to return to America, my Japanese counterpart, Otaki-san, invited me to see the Japanese parent company's plant in Mihara, where he had been plant manager for 32 years. I realized the invitation represented a great honor and accepted enthusiastically. When we arrived at the plant, I was amazed for two reasons. First, the plant was one of the largest in the parent family and made a variety of products—from locomotives to printing presses. Second, the incumbent manager had left the city for a day so Otaki-san could have the run of the plant. This respect for Otaki-san's work and position was not lost on me.

That evening, Otaki-san invited me to his favorite Geisha house. I was pleased to be included for the evening and could see the relationship between my host and the women was one that had endured for years. I did not contemplate what the nature of Otaki-san's association with the Geishas had been or was—tonight I only witnessed the affection of long-time friends. After dinner and a few rounds of drinks, Otaki-san turned to me and said, "Despain-san, I think it's time to go to bed." I nodded, drained the last of my Saki, and left the room.

When I got to my hotel room, I realized it was only 9:00 P.M. "Jeez, if I go to bed now, I'll be up at two in the morning," I thought. So I grabbed my suit coat and headed back to the dining room. Otaki-san and his favorite Geisha were still visiting, so I joined them. Otaki-san ordered another drink for me. We hardly spoke as we sipped our Saki. After an uneasy half-hour, Otaki-san repeated, "Despain-san, I think it's time to go to bed." Once again, I dutifully said my goodnights, and like a child who's not ready to leave his parents' dinner party, returned to my room. Just as I draped my jacket over a chair, I heard a knock on the door. When I opened it, there stood a young Japanese lady in a kimono.

"Despain-san," she said, "I understand you requested to have your pants pressed."

I was surprised, but a little light-headed from the Saki. "Yes, of course," I said. I closed the door, removed my trousers, and passed them to the young lady.

I sat down and contemplated what had just happened. A blinding flash of the obvious caused me to slap my forehead and smile. Otaki-san wanted to be alone with his old friend. Removing my pants ensured no more interruptions would occur. I chuckled at how tactfully Otaki-san had manipulated me. Rather than being insulted, I found myself amused with the simple subtlety of Otaki-san's gesture and was reminded of my respect for him.

The next day at breakfast, Otaki-san asked me if I had ever been to Hiroshima. I knew Hiroshima was a significant sidetrack on the way home to Tokyo. I wondered a bit why Otaki-san wanted to take me there, but concluded it was simply an act of friendship. A bit uneasy, I agreed to the trip. Otaki-san promptly sent people after tickets, and the two of us left for Hiroshima. Along the way, conversation was limited as I wondered how I would react to visiting Peace Park, the epicenter of the atomic bomb drop, with Otaki-san. First, we went to the museum. Inside, I was shocked by agonizing pictures of people and animals taken just moments after the atomic bomb was dropped. Never before had

I understood the horrific impact of the bomb. Skin seared off of the animals still standing in the picture. Prints of kimonos burned into flesh. Devastation and desolation. Around me, Japanese schoolchildren studied remnants of the massacre. From time to time, they would look at my American stature and face. I wondered what they were thinking. Were they blaming me for this terrible act? Did they find a natural hatred welling up inside them because of what America did to this city and its people? Or were they simply curious that a Westerner would even be in a place that the Japanese people saw as the final humiliation of the war? After touring the museum, Otaki-san and I walked to the eternal flame and saw the corner of the bank building with a darkened shape of a man still imprinted on the bank steps. Throughout the entire visit, we did not speak, nor did we look in one another's eyes.

When the visit was over, we returned to the train station and boarded the train for Tokyo. During the first hour of the trip, neither of us spoke. Finally, I saw something out the window and brought it to Otaki-san's attention. Our normal conversation returned, but there were no comments about the experience we had just shared. During the period of silence, I sympathized with the pain the atomic bomb inflicted on the Japanese, but I was a bit annoyed at the object lesson. War was war, and people did inhuman things during these kinds of conflicts. I wasn't proud that Truman chose to drop the bomb, but I also realized an invasion of Japan with its steep and forbidding cliffs would have cost both sides hundreds of thousands of lives. I reconciled this inner conflict with my friend by dismissing the visit as a way for Otaki-san to express the dismay the war brought to the Japanese people. I was sure this sharing was a manifestation of deep friendship. During the months that followed, neither of us mentioned the trip. There was no question, however, that our friendship continued to deepen.

Several months later, because of a product-engineering problem, Otaki-san and I needed to return to headquarters in the United States for discussions. Before making arrangements for the trip, Otaki-san approached me with a plea to stop in Los Angeles rather than travel from Tokyo to Chicago nonstop. Otaki-san told me the long flight was difficult for him because of his age and health. I told him I had no objection to stopping, but had another suggestion. "Let's stop in Honolulu instead," I said. Otaki-san agreed, and the flights were arranged. The layover in Honolulu gave us almost a full afternoon of rest before dinner. After dinner, Otaki-san suggested we meet in the lobby at noon the following day. Departure for Chicago was scheduled around 3:00 P.M. "I have a better idea," I said. "I would like you to meet me for breakfast at 8:00, and after we eat I would like to take you on a sightseeing trip."

The next morning we ate breakfast quietly. I had arranged for a trip to Pearl Harbor. We remained silent as the tour boat skipped across the white waters of the harbor, heading for the stark white edifice that straddled the remains of the battleship *Arizona*. As the boat docked, all the tourists became quiet. In between the sound of water slapping against the dock, murmurs of condolence and soft crying could be heard. We joined the others and reverently walked up the steps to the first of three sections of the memorial. The flags of the United States, Hawaii, and the Department of the Interior stood in silent tribute opposite the colors of the lost ships. As we moved into the assembly area, we could clearly see the rusting hulk of the *Arizona*. From gun turret three, small bubbles of black oil wafted to the surface. Legend has it these are the "black tears of the *Arizona*," which will continue to seep to the surface until its last survivor dies. Otaki-san and I looked both forward and aft. Parts of the huge ship protruded above the surface in stark contrast to the peaceful blue waters of the harbor. Finally, we walked to the Shrine Room. Etched in somber gray-white marble were the names of all who had died in the attack. Lines of black letters filled the entire wall, stark reminders of the nearly 2,400 victims. To the lower left of the wall, we saw a smaller white box. Here were etched the names of the *Arizona* survivors who had died since the war. In death, these men were brought back to be interred with their crewmen in gun turret number two, below the soft rhythm of the harbor's waters. The significance of the memorial sifted silently among all who stood on its floating deck. We remained still.

Time drifted away, and we boarded the tour boat back to the island. We moved toward the back of the boat where no one else was sitting, arranged ourselves on the wooden boat benches, and remained quiet. We had not spoken since leaving the shore to visit the memorial. As the boat headed back to the island, Otaki-san uncharacteristically placed his hand on my leg, an unusual entry into individual space by a Japanese person. "Despain-san," he said. "You made your point." On the rest of the trip, we kept silent, pondering the horrors our countries had committed in the name of power and dominance—and appreciating the calm and cooperation we had come to know as friends and coworkers.

Things continued to go well for me in Japan over the next few months. I enjoyed the culture and the people I worked with. I felt at peace. I considered it one of the happiest times of my life. Then, in January of my sixth year in the country, I received a call from an executive vice president of the company. He was visiting the joint venture in Japan and asked me to come to his hotel room on Sunday afternoon. I was a little apprehensive, as I didn't know exactly what he wanted. But I put on a tie and headed to the hotel. When I got to his room, he offered me the job of president of the company's new venture in Mexico. "I can't put a date on when it'll happen, Jim," he told me. "We're still negotiating with the government of Mexico and the joint venture partner. We can't announce anything until things are farther along. But it's a great opportunity for you. Congratulations."

It was a great opportunity for me, I was convinced. And I was excited to be selected for such a big job. Still, it was hard to keep the news to myself. Another coworker in Japan had lived in Mexico for several years and spoke occasionally about the culture and how much he enjoyed it. I yearned to ask him more questions, but knew I had to keep this secret to myself. So I tried to put Mexico and my new responsibilities out of my mind. I trusted that everything would be okay.

Finally, in June, the company announced its new joint venture and my position as president. My stint in Japan was over. Although happy to return to take on another new challenge, I felt a sense of deep sadness in leaving these disciplined and respectful people. The night before my departure, I celebrated my friendship with many of my fellow Japanese workers. Saki flowed freely, and laughter and cheers of "Bonsai!" punctuated the festivities. Now, it was almost time to leave my office. I spent the morning tidying up my affairs and making sure all was in order for my replacement. As I prepared to leave, I could not understand why the Japanese were not stopping in to say goodbye. My office window was frosted, and I could not see out. I felt conspicuous walking to the door to see if anyone might be coming. So I simply sat at my desk until the hour of departure. "Maybe we had too much of a party," I thought to myself. Time wore on, and still none of the people I knew and worked with came to see me. "How odd," I thought. "Maybe as a stoic people, once they say goodbye it is over." I shrugged my shoulders, packed papers in my attaché case, and prepared to make my last journey out of the office to where my chauffeur would be waiting.

I exited my office and was overwhelmed with what I saw. Along both sides of the aisle, down the long hallway, through the next office, and down the stairs, my Japanese friends and coworkers stood side by side. As I walked by them, they silently bowed, never saying a word. I wanted to say something to my friends. I wanted to let them know how much I had learned from them. I wanted to tell them how much I cared for them. But I could not speak. Tears flowed from my eyes.

***

The most penetrating recognition I ever received was not delivered by brass bands or bountiful words. No, the message delivered by the Japanese who stood in silence was more profound and moving than words could ever be. And so was my experience in this distant land where common understanding built a culture of performance and respect. New responsibilities now took me to vastly different places, so these quiet lessons lay dormant for many years, but I did not forget.

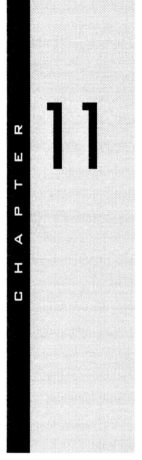

ALONE WITH MY FEARS

The fearful Unbelief is unbelief in yourself.

—THOMAS CARLYLE

For the first eight months of my new assignment—before moving to Mexico—my family and I lived in Illinois, near the company's headquarters where I worked. I returned to work confident and anxious to try out some of the leadership and people skills I had gained in Japan. I was excited about the opportunity to use what I'd learned. "What a difference this could make here!" I thought.

My eagerness and hopes, however, were quickly dashed. Although I had visited the States during our six years in Japan, until we moved back I didn't realize how assimilated to Japanese culture I had become. The contrast between our "new" U.S. home and Japan was so severe I began to feel insecure and uneasy almost immediately. The social order and respect that had become part of my natural routine suddenly vanished, replaced by brawling individualism. My fellow managers were louder and more demanding than those in Japan had been. The idea of consensus or constancy of purpose that had distinguished the Japanese culture was not visible. Respect was something demanded by leaders, often extorted from followers by threats or punishment. It was not the quiet, dutiful deference the Japanese showed to those who had position and higher responsibility. No, the Western form of respect was often fear-based, like the respect shown by a puppy for a rolled-up newspaper. I felt lost in this environment, out of sync with my fellow managers, and at the same time out of sync with myself. What was I to do with all I had learned in Japan? Abandon it? Force it on those I worked with? Instead of taking a step forward into my new job, I felt as if I were moving sideways or backward. In my confusion, I put this internal conflict out of my mind and buried myself in my job responsibilities.

My new assignment was providing leadership for the construction of a manufacturing plant in Mexico. I was excited about the job at first—and flattered beyond belief. I was only 43 years old. I didn't have a college education. Yet higher management believed I was capable of handling this responsibility. But reality began to settle in as I learned more about my new job. For the first time in its history, the company had taken a minority position in a joint venture. As president, I would report to the Mexican partner, not to the company. Construction of the facility would be handled by Mexican contractors. Only a limited number of expatriates would accompany me to Mexico. My job was to manage the building of the new plant, handle negotiations with the Mexican government, assemble a staff of Americans to assist the Mexicans with constructing and operating the factory, and hire and manage the Mexican workers who would build the products. Negotiations with the government and joint-venture partner required frequent, sometimes weekly, trips to Mexico City. Day in and day out, I dealt with people I did not know and hundreds of details I had never addressed before. I worked late and long, slept little, ate poorly, and didn't exercise. Many nights I didn't go home until after midnight.

I thought back to my first day on this new job. Confident and excited, I had smiled and said to my boss, "I won't let you down!" His response had startled me. "If we want you to succeed," he said, "you will succeed. If we want you to fail, you will fail." Now his menacing words were coming back to haunt me. I began to feel this job was beyond my abilities and out of my control. I felt alone and unsupported. I didn't know how to build a plant, let alone participate in borrowing money needed to finance one. I had never negotiated with the government of a foreign country. I had no experience in any of these matters, and I was receiving no guidance or direction from my superiors. Nor did I have layers of seasoned managers below me. After six years in Japan, my connections with the company's "network" had withered. I had no one to turn to for guidance as I coordinated the multitude of activities and assembled a team of people who would help me plan, construct, and occupy the new facility. My learning curve was steep, yet I didn't ask questions or express my concerns for fear they would reveal my inadequacies. I was sure that leaders who did were relegated to lower-level jobs or distant locations and were never heard from again. I would not become one of those people, I told myself.

But still I worried. "If we want you to fail, you will fail," rung in my ears. I began to fear that my every word and action were being watched and judged. Although I had sharpened my grammar and diction, I worried that my words were being mocked and twisted. I wondered if other managers were talking about me and what they were saying. For the first time, I felt my lack of a college education might be used against me.

As weeks turned into months, I felt a strange sensation creeping into my life. At first, I just felt jumpy. "Too much coffee," I thought to myself. "Not enough sleep. I can handle it." But little by little, the world started closing in on me. A burden without a name anchored itself to me, like the chains Marley wore in Dickens' *A Christmas Carol*. Sometimes I could feel the weight bearing down on me, pushing my thoughts into a panic, causing my heart to pound and my hands to tremble. I fought this sinister anxiety almost constantly. Sometimes it would come in the middle of a meeting, and I would have to make an excuse to leave. Sometimes I would have to pull the car over to the side of the road. But I continued to work, every day heading to the office and continuing the process of setting up the Mexican facility. I rationalized that my paranoid symptoms were "normal" in high-level positions. It was the responsibility and stress of the job. It was the long hours. It was lack of sleep. It would all change once project planning was complete and the family moved to Mexico.

After eight months, the time came to relocate. Here I can start over, I told myself. Here I will be in charge, with no one watching me or questioning me or second-guessing my decisions. Mexico itself seemed an appropriate setting for my personal and professional struggles. The country was a study in ambiguity and opposition. The architectural magnificence of the ancient Aztec builders was in contrast to the cruel practice of human sacrifice by their leaders. Reverence for the Virgin Mary and her compassion for the suffering was in contrast to the violence with which the conquistadors had pressed the natives into Christianity. Imbalance seemed inescapable in this arid land. Even the native plant, the maguey, had a strange duality. It offered sustenance as a vegetable and flavor as a vinegar. But when fermented, it was potent liquor that created an artificial euphoria and visionary hallucinations for those who sipped it.

Into this world my family and I arrived. The factory was located 100 miles south of the U.S. border, and I had insisted that all 51 Americans who worked at the joint venture live in Mexico. The living conditions at first were terrible. Homes lacked running water and reliable electricity. Landlords felt no responsibility to maintain or upgrade the structures. As renters, we had to pay for improvements or repairs needed to make the places livable. So the company converted the rental properties, investing thousands of dollars. Even so, the homes had running water only part of the time, and electricity was unpredictable. My wife and I moved into a beautiful new house where nothing worked. During our first days in the home, Gloria was nearly hit on the head when the bathroom exhaust fan suddenly fell from the ceiling. We had water piped into our home only four hours a day, two days a week. The balance of the time, the city water system was shut down because it leaked so badly.

All of the American families experienced various degrees of culture shock. I worried about my workers and their families. There were quite a few teenagers in the group, and I knew from

my own youth how easy it was to get into trouble at that age—
and how harsh the punishment in Mexico could be. People arrested even for petty crimes were usually thrown into jail, and
the American principle of innocent until proven guilty was not
the law here. To protect our families, I befriended a police officer, gave him some of my own money, and asked him to keep an
eye on us. "If there's ever an American arrested," I told him,
"please let me know right away so I can come and help." My decision paid off two times. Once, an employee leaving Mexico to
return to Illinois accidentally killed a child who ran in front of
his car. Another time, the teenage son of an employee shot a
pellet gun through the open window of a pick-up truck, hitting
the driver in the neck and causing him to run off the road into
a ditch. In both cases, the American was arrested, and I was no-
tified by the police officer. After complex negotiations, the Americans were released.

On top of these issues, problems at home compounded my
unrest. After our return to the United States from Japan, my
wife, Gloria, had undergone a mastectomy. While she was recovering, her mother and then her father both died tragically of
cancer. For two years, Gloria was lost to grief and depression—
and as her spirits declined, so did my own. I felt guilty for con-
centrating on work when she needed me at home, and equally
guilty for spending time at home when I knew so much needed
to be done at the office. The pressure became too much for me,
and I found myself reverting to the old behaviors I had learned
under Howard. I bellowed orders. I demanded results. I unleashed my temper when my expectations weren't met. I re-
sorted to any behaviors that proved effective in achieving my
objectives. I found myself changing. I knew something was happening to me, and I didn't like it. But I couldn't stop it. As I became more and more autocratic in my approach with people, I
found I was losing the serenity I had known in Japan.

Although an emerging market that longed to be part of in-
dustrialized North America, Mexico seemed confused. I found
early on that starting a company in Mexico involved multiple
trips to government officials, high-ranking businessmen,
bankers, lawyers, and more government officials. There was no
easy way to expedite the process. I figured I must have made 100

visits to people of influence in the Mexican government before the company was stable and effective. While Mexico was hungry for new industry, it still clung to the old parochialism of its Spanish heritage. No foreign industry could own a controlling interest in a Mexican company. In fact, minority ownership (at most 49 percent) was the law. This legal requirement was the reason I reported initially to the Mexican partners. To their credit, they gave me the latitude I needed to get the business up and running, but the volatility of the leadership and environment of both the Mexican corporate world and the government loomed over me like a great condor ready to swoop down on the new venture.

Also waiting in the darkness to attack me were my silent and insidious fears. Instead of getting better after the move, my symptoms got worse. I was driven to accomplish the task I had been assigned. In my heart it had to be done in spite of any difficulties, in spite of any burden it caused me personally. But I found out there was a limit. I suffered extraordinary anxiety and came close to a nervous breakdown. As best I could, I continued with my work but was painfully aware that I was falling short of my own capabilities. I don't think others recognized this to the extent that I did as my confidence continued to deteriorate. Little did I know at the time that I would suffer from this psychological intrusion for three long years.

* * *

I learned that many people suffer from similar feelings, but that didn't help me. I was told by one doctor that perhaps 20 million Americans suffer from some form of the anxiety and depression I was experiencing. I now believe that the pain I experienced was a product of a very difficult work environment, one that was filled with fear of all kinds. Some, certainly, was generated by my shortcomings. But most was generated by leaders whose focus was on intimidation and punishment, coming down hard on people whenever they thought things were a little bit wrong or took a little bit long. Encouragement and support were seemingly lost.

After my anxiety attacks abated and the "ugly demon" was gone, I asked myself, "How many other leaders within the organization and beyond have experienced something similar?" I wondered how they handled it, particularly as it related to their own performance. Later I would discover the answer. Fear and conflict in the workplace diminish people and cause two reactions. Some leaders minimize anxiety by "decoupling" and finding what I call a psychological safe zone. They don't make waves. They don't really make a difference, either. They do just what is required to get by. Others, like myself, are still driven to achieve. They plow forward and suffer the emotional and physical consequences in varying degrees. In both cases, the organization is the loser. It is ironic that many of the best leaders are sensitive, caring people—and thus are the most vulnerable. When the organization fails to support them, it is these leaders whose leadership we lose.

***

These months before the Mexican plant was up and running were ones of loneliness, extreme loneliness. I had lost the peaceful harmony of the Japanese, the unity of purpose and quiet, deep respect. I had lost the infrastructure and camaraderie that helped our U.S. industry grow. My familiar world was gone. Fear of failure ruled, bringing me physical symptoms and emotional pain. Gone was the leader who had thrived in a culture of encouragement. In his place was a man who pounded the table, demanded results, and intimidated others. In his place was a lonely autocrat who once again "delivered the goods," but what a price I paid! Eight years later, an even greater business challenge would be placed before me, but because of this experience I would be open to new methods—I would find a better way.

EXCELLENCIA

It is a funny thing about life;
if you refuse to accept anything but the best,
you very often get it.

—SOMERSET MAUGHAM*

inally, the day came for hiring the workforce to run our magnificent factory. For me it marked the end of lamenting the loss of a positive culture in Japan and the beginning of building one of our own in Mexico. But this, too, was a challenge. It wasn't that the people of Mexico weren't intelligent and capable. They were. But their poverty, culture, and education did not produce the skills necessary for this great endeavor. Would-be workers often had the mechanical aptitude to work the heavy manufacturing equipment, but they had no mechanical experience. They were like children who knew how a bicycle worked—pedal, steer, glide—but had never ridden one. Very often, the Mexicans came from lives where they had to "make do" just to

---

*Permission granted from the estate of Elizabeth Lady Glendevon.

stay alive or provide for their families. This make-do existence never exposed them to opportunities requiring excellence. It was a concept that had not been defined for them through their own life experiences. Quality, excellence, and achievement were strangely foreign to a people whose history included the wonders of the Mayan, Incan, and Aztec cultures.

This apparent lack of alignment with the work expectations of the American parent troubled me. The new company could not produce substandard quality simply because it was located in Mexico. How could these expectations be infused into an undereducated workforce? How could my team and I expect those who had no mechanical experience and had experienced a life of poverty to overcome the poor work habits and attitudes that had been etched in their minds? There was only one way, I decided. We would have to create our own workforce from people who had not been tainted by experience in other industries. We would choose only the best and the brightest. We would make the plant a work haven where people felt privileged to be part of the company. We would accept only excellence on every front. We would not waver from this concept—*excellencia,* as it was called in Spanish—or the new company would be doomed.

"Excellencia," I thought, "will drive everything we do. It will become a source of pride for our people and our company."

Excellencia became a passion with me, starting with the building of the plant. I watched carefully every aspect of the project. One wall was built and torn down and built again five times, another painted six times. I was relentless in my pursuit of perfection. Sidewalks, plumbing, landscaping—it didn't matter, it was done well or it was done over. I recognized early in the project that in this culture I had to establish and exert my authority. My towering height and deep, bellowing voice once again became my most important management tools. Still, I was astute enough to recognize the duality of the people—authority without sensitivity could lead to a revolt. I made sure that when the job was done right, people were praised and rewarded. I let people know I did not carry a grudge. And so the American gringo got his plant built.

And what a plant it was. The factory was a gleaming tribute to the 3,000 construction workers who at one time or another left their fingerprints on the job. In building the plant, my team and I did another important thing. We showed the people who worked there that the new management team valued them in the pursuit of excellencia. Amenities uncommon to most of Mexico were built for the employees. A large recreational area for families was completed with an Olympic-size swimming pool, basketball court, soccer field, baseball diamond, and jogging track. Polapas were scattered around the field and provided a pleasant place for picnics and cookouts. Flowers, beautiful pink and red hibiscus, and many other flowering plants added color, grace, and serenity to the park.

As the plant neared completion, we began the difficult process of hiring. "Remember," I told the human relations staff, "excellencia." The vast majority of new applicants were not acceptable for any number of reasons. But mostly it was because they could not grasp the concept of excellencia. The new company found it necessary to hire young people who had no preconceived notions of quality. People were avoided who had worked for any length of time for industries where quality had not been a primary issue. Laboriously we worked our way through thousands of applications. In the end, only two to three percent of those who wanted to work at the big American plant were hired. The average age of the eventual 1,500 employees—including 25 American managers—was 21. We had hired a young, unspoiled, eager workforce.

Once the workforce was in place, we wasted no time impressing upon them the importance of excellencia. As the plant was being prepared for the leaders of the Mexican company to inspect, I found that someone had left a hammer on the beautiful mahogany conference table in the administrative conference room. I had previously told the management team that excellencia had to start in the office of the president. The new office had to be a reflection of the excellencia being pursued. When I saw the hammer and a scratch on the table near it, I was reminded of these directions.

I immediately summoned the supervisor of the maintenance organization. "Carlos," I said.

"Yes, Señor Despain?" Carlos answered.

"Carlos, this is not excellencia," I said, pointing to the scratch. "This must be fixed. It must be perfect."

Anxious to please his new American boss and wary of my authority, Carlos answered, "Sí, Señor Despain. I will attend to it today."

The next morning, I inspected the table. It was beautifully refinished. The scratch was invisible. I was pleased and relieved until I looked at the carpeting below the table. There, beside the table, drops of varnish speckled the carpet.

"Carlos!" I summoned the man again. "Come with me. Look here at the floor." Carlos looked down, but didn't see what my problem was. "Carlos, do you see the spots on this carpet?"

"Sí, Señor Despain. The woodworkers must have spilled a little when they fixed the table."

"Carlos, the table is excellencia. The carpet is not. Please fix the carpet."

Carlos promised to get the carpet cleaned that afternoon. Later in the day, I returned to check. The carpet looked brand new. Relieved and pleased that Carlos was catching on, I turned to leave and couldn't believe my eyes. There were heel marks all over the wall. Apparently the carpet cleaner had scraped his work boots against the freshly painted wall while he was on his knees cleaning the carpet. Now black skid marks marred the otherwise perfect room.

Once again, I called Carlos in, but before I could say anything, Carlos scrutinized the room. "The heel marks, Señor Despain. They are not excellencia. I will have the wall repainted." I nodded my approval and slapped Carlos on the back.

"Carlos," I said proudly, "knowing that the wall is not excellencia is excellencia. It is this kind of attention we need to give everything we do."

A bit confused, but happy he had gotten it right, Carlos nodded. "I will make sure the room is perfect for our guests. I am beginning to understand what it is that creates excellencia." Although my patience was beginning to wear thin, I inwardly celebrated this small victory. I knew Carlos would be an evangelist for my ideas on quality. "Each one, teach one," I thought to myself. "That's how we're going to make this plant successful. Today is a beginning."

I knew from my experience in Japan that devotion to quality was almost like a religion. People had to believe with passion that it was important. People had to relate to it on a personal level. People had to practice it every minute of every day. I was not going to let the lesson Carlos learned be an isolated one. We began an extensive training program for all employees, and as time went on, the entire family was included. Beyond the regular skills of the job, the company offered classes that helped create excellencia in each worker's personal life as well—classes on general health, prenatal care, cooking, parenting, fitness, anything that improved the health and well-being of the workforce. Still, education in excellencia was not enough. People had to practice it. People had to be reminded.

We began holding monthly all-employee meetings. Before the meetings, we would send a photographer through the office and the plant. There the photographer would capture a person at his or her workstation while at work. Then the photographer captured each worker in another picture, smiling, perhaps giving a thumbs-up or "number one" gesture. At the end of each all-employee meeting, the lights would dim and festive Latin music would begin to play. Across the slide screen came the faces of the people of the plant and their family members in classes or enjoying recreation at the sports field or in the polapas. The slides were placed in a kind of collage that showed the employee working first and then smiling at the camera. Family members were included as they were involved in various classes or recreational events. At first, the Mexican workers were surprised to see themselves and not the executives of the organization in the presentation. Then they began to realize that they too played a most important role in the success of the company. After a few minutes the lights were turned on, and in almost every all-employee meeting, the short photography experience brought tears to the young workers' eyes. Each time, I would announce in a booming voice, "This is excellencia. This is excellencia!" Across the faces of the audience spread pride—and often more tears and an explosion of applause. Excellencia would become second nature to the Mexican plant.

Things were moving ahead superbly for us. The plant was doing well, and the company was pleased. Then in 1982, a financial crisis hit Mexico. The parent Mexican company suffered serious cash flow problems and was forced to sell its interest in the new company. I began making presentations across the country in an effort to find a new partner. But the investment capital required was high, and no Mexican company was willing to take the risk. Sadly, we began laying off workers after barely two years of existence. I watched as 20 technical apprentices received diplomas for graduating from a technical apprentice program and two days later were laid off. "We prepared them, we taught them, and someone else will get their expertise," I thought. We went on a rampage of meetings, convinced a new investor could be found. But as the rejections mounted, it was obvious the American parent would have to achieve government approval to own 100 percent of the company—no easy task, since Mexican law forbid foreign companies from owning more than 49 percent. So we began a long series of meetings with Mexican government officials to negotiate 100 percent ownership, a process that eventually required more than 100 trips to Mexico City. But our persistence paid off. After six months of negotiations, the government allowed the American company to purchase the plant outright. We were back in business. We immediately started recalling the workforce and continued the focus on excellencia.

My tough exterior and unyielding demands for quality were reinforced by the plant's performance. Quality was second to none of the plants in the United States. Soon, the company moved the production of lift trucks from the United States to the Mexican plant. We were worried about our untrained and inexperienced workforce maintaining the standards for quality set at the American location. But when the first reports came in, we saw the Mexican team had reduced the number of defects per truck after assembly to 50 percent of what it had been in the American plant. This level of quality was maintained for the entire period of production. "This is excellencia!" I said to no one but myself, then raised my fist high above my head and let it drop to the table in a thunderous hit, celebrating and savoring the accomplishment.

I found the naivete of the work force combined with their newfound commitment to excellencia proved a powerful force. Time and time again, the Mexican workers responded to my aggressive leadership with a tremendous sense of urgency and the ability to learn quickly. They took on a variety of new work and through tireless efforts reduced lead times to unprecedented levels. And because they were unfettered in their mindset and committed to delivering the excellencia the company demanded, they made things happen.

***

The combination of quality and "all things are possible" thinking made a solid impression on me. I realized that lofty goals coupled with seemingly impossible deadlines thoroughly energized achievement. I started to understand why men climbed Mount Everest or went to the moon or tried to break land-speed records. Why? Because they believed in excellence and because they believed in themselves. They knew they could achieve it. "This power," I thought to myself, "can create an unmatchable competitive edge. I will remember this."

13

BACK TO THE BEGINNING

I never give them hell.
I just tell the truth and they think it's hell.

—HARRY S TRUMAN*

E ight years after I began the Mexican assignment, I was called home. I felt an unusual sadness. Getting the plant up and running, then losing the momentum, and then seeing it rise again like the mythical Phoenix was unique in my business experiences. I realized my sadness stemmed from being pulled away from the journey the Mexican plant was taking in building its reputation, its work culture, and its future. It was as if I had started out the skipper of a sailboat with a group of people I'd never met and who knew little about sailing. Together we learned to stay the course, navigate through dangerous shoals, sail through smooth waters, and weather small and gigantic storms. A new assignment in the United States made me feel as if I had

---

*Permission granted from the Harry S Truman Library.

been put ashore. I was happy to have my feet on solid ground again, but part of me still longed to sail with the crew and to see where the journey would take us.

While leaving Mexico at this juncture saddened me, I wasn't completely disappointed in my next assignment. In fact, I was excited about the prospect of coming home, of returning as plant manager of the factories where I had begun my career with the company as a sweeper more than 33 years before. Soon after returning home, I drove my wife around the plant in our car to show her the breadth of my new responsibility. "My God," was Gloria's reaction. She was stunned by the sheer size of the plant and the massive number of people who worked inside.

But more exciting to me than size and scope was that this plant was known by many as the company's crown jewel—the mother ship. It built the company's signature equipment, the equipment from which the company took its name. I knew the quality of the product that came out of the plant. "The best in the company," I thought to myself. "At least here we'll have a jump start on excellencia!" This quality helped generate a commanding lead in worldwide market share. "This is good. As markets mature here at home, we're making up the difference in Europe and Asia. This is good." I knew the managers at the plant. "Well-seasoned, most experienced, know the business, good team." The manufacturing processes in the plant had just been modernized. This too buoyed my spirits as I prepared for my return and to make an impact in my new position.

During my first days back at the plant, I expected to feel a sense of nostalgia, a homecoming of sorts. But instead things seemed somehow distorted or out of kilter. And as the days stretched into weeks, and my involvement as plant manager grew, I felt more and more like a stranger in a strange land. Nowhere did I see the calm respect of the Japanese or the strong sense of teamwork I had grown to love and admire in Mexico. Nowhere did I see the quiet progress of *kaizen* or the enthusiasm of excellencia. Instead, I saw managers and workers pushing for control and testing limits. I saw informers and scapegoats. I saw political-like favors being curried and granted. Intrigue, ambush, attack, retreat—this was the daily routine of the plant. In fact, so much energy was expended in the power struggle that I often wondered how any work ever got done.

One day, I heard that Frank, one of my department managers, had given a strange order. Apparently, he had noticed a factory worker spending an extended period of time away from his workstation. He checked in the restroom and, with some effort, managed to look over a stall door. Inside, the worker sat reading a newspaper. As a result, Frank gave an order for all the building's restroom doors to be cut in half.

I called Frank into my office. "Is it true you've given an order to cut the restroom doors in half?"

"Crap, Jim, you know these slackers. We've got to watch them everywhere. I just made it a little easier to check up on them," Frank replied.

"Do you think cutting off the bathroom doors is an appropriate response?" I barked. "Do you think it's fair to make everyone pay for one guy's offense?"

"You're damn right," Frank answered. "People have gotten the message, and you don't see newspapers all over the floor anymore."

"Frank, I don't want you or anybody else checking on people when they're in the can. For Pete's sake, we've got to respect the privacy of our people. Replace the doors and do it now."

"Hell, Jim, they don't deserve privacy. Give 'em privacy and they'll sit around all day reading the newspaper."

I felt the veins in my neck throbbing. "Frank, are you going to put the doors back on, or am I?" I asked in a much louder and more authoritarian voice than I had used in a long time.

"I can't believe you're sticking up for those guys," Frank said.

"I'm not sticking up for anybody. It's about decency and privacy." My patience was wearing thin and my tone of voice reflected it. "Now what are you going to do about those doors?"

"All right, all right, I'll put the doors back up," Frank said. "But if we run into problems with slackers in the future, don't come crying to me."

The doors went back up. The ire that Frank's act had caused subsided temporarily. But the peace was shattered when a man was found sleeping on a stool in the tool room, while his machine ran idly without turning out a piece of work. This time Frank ordered the removal of every stool in the tool room. He didn't care whether the stools were necessary for some of the employees to do their work or not. Sitting on a stool meant the opportunity to sleep—and Frank wanted none of that. Again, he punished everyone for the act of a single individual. Again, his solution generated anger and complaints from the workforce. Again, I intervened. The stools went back.

Skirmishes like these continued on a routine basis. Some workers wanted to do a good job, but knew their coworkers might threaten or embarrass them for doing so. Others had taken advantage of the company for years, doing as little as they could to get by. Managers and supervisors generally fell into one of two camps. One group walked a fine line between the workers they supervised and the management group that supervised them. Most had been burnt on both sides trying to do their jobs and were simply afraid to do much of anything extraordinary anymore. In the second group were the "bull of the woods" managers. They thrived on conflict in the plant, taking pleasure in stirring the pot and squaring off at one another. Once, I heard one of these managers say to another, "I didn't sleep too good last night, and I don't feel so great this morning. I'm going to go get my adrenaline up—I'm going to go find somebody to chew the hell out of to get my heart started."

All these experiences reminded me of my time in the plant some 30 years before. I remembered pushing my broom and listening to supervisors harass the workers. "You stupid SOB...what kind of a moron...your ass is outta here...." I remembered my excitement at running a machine beyond its listed capacity and receiving threats from my coworkers. "A man could get beaten up pretty bad if he's not careful...don't piss off the boys or you'll regret it..."

"But that was 30 years ago," I thought. "I've changed. Why haven't they?"

***

After the restroom and tool-room incidents, I began applying rules consistently in the plant. I supported supervisors who were trying to do their jobs. Often, management gave in to the complaints of front-line workers without hearing the supervisor's side of the story. It wasn't that management believed the worker more than the supervisor—it was just more expedient to give in to the worker and avoid the whole grievance issue. So what if supervisors were made scapegoats? Someone had to take the heat, so it might as well be them. But this practice not only created an environment lacking in integrity, it also destroyed any semblance of discipline, policy, and purpose there might have been. I knew this automatic direction of blame toward line supervisors was not good for the company. Who would want to be a supervisor, knowing that when trouble came, you were always wrong? Who would want to follow the rules, knowing management would take the worker's side over yours any day? The habit bred fear and hatred. I did my best to stop it. Consistency in the application of policy and support of supervisors began to pay off. Politicking diminished. Backbiting and blaming began to be less harsh. I felt I was making progress in the plant.

After several successful months as plant manager, I attended a Plant Operations Council meeting, where all the managers, plant managers, and officers of the company gathered to discuss strategy and plans for the future. After dinner one evening during the week-long session, two other managers and I were playing cards with Roger, the chairman of the company.

"Get up for a minute, Jim, and come over here and talk to me," Roger said.

I was a little worried. Did I make some mistake in the game? I wondered as I followed Roger to an isolated area.

"If I submit your name to the board of directors to become an officer of the company, to become vice president of North American plants, would you accept?" Roger asked.

I about fell out of my skin. I was floored. Vice president of North American plants! The promotion was heady. Now I would have responsibility for all the plants in the United States, the plant in Canada, and the plant in Mexico. Now I would have the position and authority to try some of the ideas I had discovered in Japan and Mexico. The opportunity was mind-boggling. "Of course," I stammered to Roger. "Of course."

I felt as if I were floating on air the rest of the evening. When I got home, I took Gloria downstairs to the bar for a glass of wine. "You know that trip Matt (a company vice president) and I are taking tomorrow?" I asked with a grin. "Well, there are going to be two vice presidents on that plane." I laughed out loud. Vice president! *This is better than a dream come true,* I thought, *because I never dreamed I'd make it this far.*

Soon after, I was officially elected vice president of North American plants. Ralph, the retiring vice president, began to break me in. He drove me from plant to plant, pointing out each facility's strengths and weaknesses. He explained which managers were worth their weight in gold and which constantly needed a "kick in the pants." I asked Ralph thousands of questions, ranging from the very high-level to the most mundane. One day, as we traveled to a plant south of headquarters, I asked, "When you go to these plants, where do you park?"

Ralph gave me a strange look. With steely eyes as cold as the iron that went into the company's product, he responded, "Anywhere I goddamn please."

I chuckled out loud so I wouldn't insult Ralph, but deep down I was knocked off balance by the answer. Somehow it conveyed the absolute power of my new position. This man Ralph could park anywhere, and no one would question him. No one in the company held a more supreme position over employees in North America than Ralph did. And soon, I realized, I would assume that power. The realization frightened me a bit. On one hand, I would have the power to make the workplace better. On the other, I stood the chance of acquiring Ralph's attitude of superiority toward the very people who made the position possible. I wondered how I could keep from going down that road. I wondered how I could adapt my power and position to create connections, not barriers, with the people I led.

I never had the opportunity to find out. Within a year, the company began to undertake a major restructuring project. The company's executives were faced with an ever-expanding business, one that was growing not only into new areas of the United

States and the world, but also into new areas of business. Financial services. Insurance. Logistics. Power generation. World trade. As the company grew, it became more and more difficult—and more and more time-consuming—to control operations from one central location. Why not, a strategic planning committee of company executives asked, create independent divisions, each with its own operations and financial responsibilities? Why not go back to the entrepreneurial style that made us successful in the past? Why not give the power to the people closest to the action, the people who know the ins and outs of their specific businesses, industries, competitors, and customers?

And so the giant company was reorganized into divisions. Some functions remained centralized, like human resources and public relations. But for the most part, the divisions were given their independence—and the responsibility to prove their worth financially. My position as vice president of North American plants was no longer needed. I was assigned to a staff vice president position at the company's headquarters, where I ostensibly provided manufacturing expertise to three of the plants I had led under my old position. But the shift was uneasy. I really had no authority—I was an adviser, a consultant. Drawing on my experiences in Mexico, I provided strong leadership in developing organizational lines of management for the plants. But creating organizational charts and assigning responsibilities wasn't an ongoing task, and it didn't take me long to complete. Soon, I found I had nothing to do, and I felt the old emotions of my first days in Japan resurfacing. Frustrated and annoyed, I went to my boss.

"Greg, we've completed the organizational work for the plants," I said, "but now it seems there's nothing left for me to do."

"Nothing to do?" Greg laughed. "C'mon, Jim, there's always plenty to do around here. You're just in a lull. Now get back to your office and see how you can help those plants."

"Maybe he's right," I thought. "After all, getting the right people in the right positions takes a lot of work. I'll give the plant managers a few more weeks and then see how I can help."

But in a few weeks, the plant managers still had no time or work for me. In the reverse situation, I wouldn't have had any for them, either. I tried to amuse myself with minor paper pushing, but it didn't help. My entire career at the company had been spent where the action was, in the plants. There, deadlines were tight and accomplishments were clear. Product rolling out the door on time and within budget was a success. Anything less was failure. That I knew how to do. I knew how to succeed and how to motivate others. Most of my career had been spent managing people. No matter that the people had been different—the rough and tough Midwest factory workers, the quiet and respectful Japanese, the young and enthusiastic Mexicans. Part of the challenge, part of the fun, had been figuring out the right way to relate to each group.

In this staff job, I had none of those things. I had little, if any, opportunity to make things happen inside the plants. I had no people to supervise, to motivate, to challenge. And without them, my demeanor turned sour. I was sullen at work and harsh at home. I looked for signs I was being set up to be let go. I began to question my ability. I wondered how I had ever been so successful. I spoke sarcastically about being the "vice president of nothing" and called my secretary the "secretary of nothing."

As the restructuring of the company neared completion, my boss called me into his office. "Jim, it's time for a more permanent assignment. There are two alternatives. You can choose."

My stomach tightened. I was being demoted. I knew it. "What are they?" I asked flatly.

"Well, it's one of two facilities or businesses," Greg said. "You will be vice president in charge of one of the new strategic divisions." Then he identified the two alternatives. "Take some time and think about where you want to go."

I saw the writing on the wall. Instead of being in charge of all the plants in North America, I was being relegated to just one. The muscles on the back of my neck tensed. I was not going to be a willing participant in this conspiracy to spiral down my career. If my superiors wanted to demote or retire me, then by God, they were going to have to do it by themselves. "I think you should make that decision based on my skills and abilities," I told Greg. "I think you should know best where I ought to go. You decide and let me know."

"Are you sure?" Greg asked.

"Yep. You decide." My words dropped with a resounding thud. For the first time in as long as I could remember, I was walking away from a decision that directly affected me. Inwardly, I shuddered. "Who have I become?"

***

Shortly after my conversation with Greg, I was named vice president and general manager of the company's Track-Type Tractors Division. I would be returning to the facility where I had begun my career as a sweeper, the facility I had returned to as plant manager just two years before. Suddenly, it didn't seem like a demotion. I was relieved with the assignment. At least I would be back in the plant, back to managing people and getting product out the door, the things I did best. Yes, the division had culture problems, but it also had the most modern and technologically advanced manufacturing processes, the highest quality products, and the most experienced management team. And now that it was an independent division, the facility also had its own profit-and-loss responsibility. "This is better than a functional responsibility for several plants without bottom-line responsibility," I thought. Now I would be able to implement some of the management techniques I'd learned over the years and show the company how profitably I could lead a division.

As I settled into my new position, my first order of business was to understand the new financial statements. Previously, this manufacturing entity had been like all other manufacturing plants, a cost center. I was anxious, but not because I was worried about the numbers. Instead, I couldn't wait to find out how much I could help improve the profitability of the division. How much more profit could the division squeeze out using the concepts I'd learned in Japan and executed in Mexico? Again, I recalled my early days as a supervisor. I remembered how I had inherited the worst-performing lines in the plant, but how together, under my leadership, they had become the most productive. My old dream of leading a team wearing matching shirts and dungarees drifted through my mind. "Finally, after all these years, it's going to happen," I told myself. I couldn't wait to get my hands on that P&L.

During this period of waiting, I reassessed the situation. The company as a whole was profitable; therefore, my new division had to be. In fact, when I considered the seasoned management capability, the state-of-the-art manufacturing technology recently implemented at a cost of several hundred million dollars, the division's reputation for quality, and its overall market performance, deep inside I thought the division might be among the top units in the company. And when I let myself dream a little, I even thought it might be the company's top performer.

Finally, the accounting people brought me the numbers. I studied them closely, looking carefully at each number and scrutinizing the bottom line. Something was terribly wrong. The numbers weren't good. In fact, they were awful. The business was bleeding red. "This can't be," I thought. "There has to be a mistake. How can we not be making money? Somebody messed up. Somebody double-counted costs or overlooked some buckets of profit."

I called the accounting people back into my office immediately. "There is something wrong with these financials. What I see is not possible. You guys missed something. Please go through them again and find the error."

The accountants were fairly certain the financials were correct, but my tone of voice left no room for argument. They left the office, saying they'd be happy to rerun the numbers.

The next day I received a new report. The numbers were exactly the same, so I requested a meeting with the division's business manager. Together we went over the figures carefully. I asked question after question and again requested the numbers be rechecked.

When the third report arrived, it was delivered by one of the younger accountants in the division. I knew from this alone that the news was bad. If there had been an error, if the financials had changed somehow, the business manager would have brought them himself. Indeed, there was little if any difference. The plant was losing money, significant money—tens of millions of dollars a year. Of this the accountants were sure.

"Damn," I thought. "No change. Deja vu. What are we going to do now?"

***

Here I was full circle, back to where I began more than 30 years ago. Back home. And home was bleeding red. Although the division also made tractors in Brazil, Japan, and France, this was the major operation; here were the largest facilities and undoubtedly the source of the problem and the key to the answer. Knowing the truth kindled my doubts. "How could we ever profitably manufacture equipment here when we had some of the highest labor rates in the world? And what might our other problems be?" I thought. My American spirit and competitive juices were crying for answers. We had work to do. We had to find a way.

TURNING IT AROUND

*Never doubt that a small group of thoughtful,
committed citizens can change the world.
Indeed, it is the only thing that ever has.*

—MARGARET MEAD

The nation—and my business unit—entered the early 1990s on a less-than-optimistic note. For the first time in over a decade, the government reported a declining economy. Unemployment topped seven percent. A confused America faced a presidential election with not two, but three viable candidates. The economy became the focus of the election. The economy also became the focus of my management team. The financial results of the division were not changing. Each monthly report only confirmed what I feared—the division was not making money. Something had to change, or there would be no tomorrow.

Out of ideas on how to turn the business around, I called our department managers together. "What are we going to do?" I asked. "Let's think about our options."

We argued and discussed all kinds of solutions—most of which had already been implemented over the past several years. Costs had been cut. Total Quality Management was in place. Concurrent product and process development had been introduced. Millions of dollars had been invested in modernizing and automating our plants. We were the market-share leader, so generating profit through sales growth was not a reasonable option. Over and over, we coursed through the standard management solutions. Time and time again, we came to the realization that nothing we were currently doing could be improved enough to resolve the problem. Exasperated, our conversation drifted in a new direction.

"You know, I wish everybody in the plant had the same kind of survival attitude we have in this room," one department manager said.

"Yeah. You know, if everyone was feeling this pain, maybe they'd want to do something to help fix it," another chimed in.

"Jeez, this situation is hopeless. I don't see how we can get out of it."

The conversation went around in circles for almost an hour. Then Gordo, one of the older and most vocal managers, began to speak. "If we continue to do what we've always done, we're going to continue to get what we've always got. We need to change the way we do things if we're going to fix this problem."

"What do you mean?" I asked. "What do you mean, change things? We just talked about all this. We've got new technology. We've improved our quality. We have a solid position in the marketplace. What else can we do?" I wasn't angry—I was desperate.

"Well, one of the things we're not doing is energizing our people," Gordo said. "We're not getting their buy-in. We don't have their trust. We're not picking their brains or unleashing their creativity. If we don't turn loose the power of our people, we're never going to make any strides in cutting costs. We can't do it alone."

I saw a glimmer of hope in Gordo's words. His ideas made sense. I remembered the threats delivered to me and others who tried to do more than was expected. I remembered the boss who didn't give me the bonus to which I was entitled and then not caring or working to make a difference. On the positive side I had seen how the Japanese built respect in people and created a culture of achievement. I had seen how a highly motivated workforce in Mexico had produced excellencia. Yes, Gordo was on to something, but how could we eliminate animosity and get people to care about the business—really care—here and now? We were aware of the negative culture that existed in the division. Leaders managing by fear and intimidation. Workers doing only what it took to get by. Union and management constantly vying for the upper hand. How, in this environment, could we possibly make people feel committed? Where should we start? I left the meeting unsure of our next steps but keenly interested in the immense potential power of people to make a positive difference and management's responsibility to create a culture that enabled them to do so.

Later that day, Gordo stopped me in the hallway. "I want you to look at something I developed for my department," he said. "It's about some of the things we discussed today." I took the piece of paper Gordo handed me. It was filled with several paragraphs of single-spaced, typewritten words. I began to read his vision for his group.

Gordo's Group Vision

Our group is an organization that is responsive, flexible, always open to new ideas, ready to explore options, willing to take risk, focused on results, and completely void of bureaucracy. Everything is open to challenge. There is a strong sense of urgency and recognition of the value and competitive advantage of time. Time is our number one discipline. Quality and costs will follow. We all focus on the customer—employees, users, plants, marketing units, and dealers. Everyone continuously asks himself or herself, "How do I, in my job, better help our customers?" The customer, in every single decision, is the arbiter.

Our management style is one of coaching, which totally embraces and utilizes the team concept. Common goals, a shared vision, and total commitment are achieved within the organization. There is always open and explicit communication from top to bottom and bottom to top. Information is shared. Trust always prevails.

A productive and creative work environment exists and high levels of personal satisfaction are achieved. People are empowered. They understand their roles and are given the freedom to accept responsibility and accountability. Risk taking is encouraged, and there is no penalty for mistakes or false starts; the emphasis is on corrective action and a learning experience for the future. Everyone is given the opportunity to identify and help solve work-related problems, continuous improvement is a way of life, and quality is recognized as being very personal. Decision making is placed at the most appropriate level, and inputs are invited from those most affected by the decision made. Everyone feels valued, involved, and contributing to the decision-making process. There is a high level of self-esteem. People enjoy coming to work, have fun performing their jobs, and see their future and growth as identical to that of the company's. Rewards and recognition reinforce this behavior and commitment.

Employees get positive feedback for the creation of developmental plans targeting areas where time should be invested in growing their skills. The performance evaluation process is based on the supervisor and employee mutually developing job responsibilities and performance standards that are aligned with our business plan; a portion of our compensation is tied to the performance of our business unit.

As I read them, the words seemed to pound in my ears: "Our management style is one of coaching.... Trust always prevails.... Risk taking is encouraged, and there is no penalty for mistakes or false starts; the emphasis is on corrective action and a learning experience for the future." I remembered with shame how I had once berated a man named Jerry who had brought me a report that I viewed as misleading and incomplete. When I realized that others were listening to my encounter with him, I repeated my degrading words, only more forcefully and loudly. It was the end of the day, so I left abruptly without giving Jerry a chance to respond, got in my car, and started home. As I began to drive I became so incensed again at what I perceived to be his errors that I returned to the plant, burst into his office, and continued dressing him down.

I felt saddened by this bitter memory. "There is no penalty for mistakes," Gordo's vision said, "the emphasis is on corrective action and a learning experience for the future." Yet I had not taught Jerry. I had ridiculed him. A warm wave of shame continued to wash over me as I realized I had become someone I did not want to be. Unless I changed, the organization would not change. I could blame others, use traditional methods, and try to muscle our problems to the ground as I had in the past, or I could view Gordo's vision as a defining moment for the organization and for me personally.

I sat quietly for several minutes as I thought, then I nodded my head and looked up at Gordo. "This vision for the culture in your department is very powerful," I said. "How long have you been using it?"

"A long time," he replied.

"Has it changed anything there?"

"Not as much as we would like," Gordo said. "But we still believe it holds the answers for us, that it is where we need to be."

"Why don't we use it throughout the whole organization?" I suggested. "Maybe then it will have more impact."

I brought Gordo's Group Vision to our next department manager meeting. "We have a vision for our business, for Caterpillar and for our division, that tells us where we want to go in the future," I said. "Having an explicit vision for our *human* organization, like Gordo's group has written, is an amazing thought. It defines how we are expected to interact with each other, how we are expected to behave as we work together to achieve the vision for our business. It defines the culture we need in order to engage employees and solve our many problems."

The department managers read the vision and liked the concept, so we decided to ask a professor from the University of Illinois to design a survey to determine how well we were doing on the items mentioned in Gordo's draft. I felt better. At least we were taking a step in the right direction. A new course of action was beginning to take form.

In a few weeks, I received a phone call from the professor. "You know, we've been working on this thing for a while, and we've run into some problems. The words and terms are so ambiguous that they can be interpreted in many ways. If you gave a survey, you wouldn't get consistent answers."

"You mean it can't be done?" I asked.

"It could, but it wouldn't tell you much. The concepts aren't well defined, so they'll probably mean different things to different people."

I was disappointed but undeterred. I met with the managers again and explained the ambiguity problem. I challenged them to create a new statement—a vision statement for our division that succinctly told people what was expected in terms of behavior.

"When people read it, they need to understand it immediately," I said. "If we need to change, we must know what to change to. We need to describe interactions and relationships with customers, suppliers, and each other. All of this must be stated so that everyone understands expectations. There must be no doubts. There must be no ambiguous statements."

We had all seen how vision statements, Gordo's included, were stuck on walls or lost in files. They were so high level, people couldn't relate to them. They were just words. They didn't tell people how to make the vision a reality. We wanted our vision to describe a human organization that was active and alive. We wanted it to clearly tell people what behaviors were expected here. We wanted it to be something we could all understand, act on, and measure. To guide our process, we met with consultants and academicians who were experts on culture change. We also held a benchmarking session with representatives from companies with culture change experience, including AT&T, NCR, Hewlett-Packard, Motorola, and GE. We learned that each company approached the task differently. What was common among them was the passion and absolute commitment these men and women had for helping their respective companies face the need to change. Above all, this commitment was the most significant lesson to be learned. But there was no miracle cure to share and no silver bullet to fire.

Disappointed but no less enthusiastic, we began to define our own journey. We put our total energy into the development of a new vision for our human organization, one that would become the blueprint for behavior in our division. For days, we wrote, discussed, analyzed, argued, and wrote again. Finally, we came to consensus. We had a concept we all liked and could support. Then came the hard part. "Are we willing to put achieving this above everything else we do here?" I asked the group. "Are we ready to make this our number-one priority? Don't be a yes-person here today. If anyone has a problem, speak now. If anyone thinks we can't do this, let's try to determine why."

The people around the table realized the gravity of these questions. We were managers. We were accountants and engineers and marketing experts. We told people what to do and evaluated them on how well they did it. We were not accustomed to being dreamers and visionaries. Still, we understood the reality of the situation. We had already used every rational business approach we knew, and the results weren't what we wanted. We knew we were going into uncharted waters. We began to recognize that we would have to leave the comfort of our management experience and enter a new dimension of leadership to make it happen.

The group sat in silence for a few minutes—heads down, hands folded. No one moved. Finally, Gordo spoke. "Let's get on with it," he said. "These are things we should have been doing all along. This is the right way to go." With the silence broken, heads began nodding. Positive responses, although a bit uneasy, spread throughout the group.

"Okay, good. This is good," I said. "Next thing we have to determine is how we get there. What has to change here for us to reach this vision?"

The question dropped like a bomb. Everyone in the room knew what an ugly environment existed in the division. But talking about it was painful, embarrassing, even threatening. We would have to open ourselves up for criticism, for blame. We would have to admit we weren't perfect leaders. We would have to reveal we had verbally embellished performance and even results. It was easy to talk about the need to change, but talking about what had to change was another story. That was personal. Our "management masks" reappeared.

"Look guys, we can't make a change if we don't open up about what needs to be changed. This isn't an indictment of who we are and what we've done," I said. "Hell, I'm probably the guiltiest of all—bellowing out orders, chewing out people in front of others, shooting the messenger. But that's going to stop. I need you to help me. We all need to help each other. We all need to be on the same page. So what's got to change?"

Tentatively the conversation began. Minor sins were confessed first. Then we started digging into bigger issues. Overwhelming bureaucracy. Superfluous activities that added nothing to the product, only to the ego of managers. Processes that made no sense. Two or three people doing jobs one person could do. Hierarchical problems that were a drain on the division and a source of contention among groups. As the list grew and grew, we began to realize the magnitude of our job. We decided to write a description, a definition, of who we really were as a division. It was a painful process. For years, we had been telling one another and the rest of the organization how good we were. For years, we had spun bad news into acceptable rhetoric—making eagles out of sparrows. For years, we had been rewarded for our performance. Now we had to admit our leadership was leaving the division far short of successful performance. The gap between who the organization was and what it wanted to become was huge.

To evaluate the gap, we drew a diagram, placing our vision in a small circle and the reality of our current organization in a large one. We drew lines between the diameters of the two circles to create a funnel. "Everything we are doing outside the funnel must be stopped," I said. "The people doing these things will no longer be needed in the organization or they need to be redirected, because they're not contributing to the journey we need to take. If we're going to go from who we are to what we want to be, we've got to stay inside the funnel."

We were concerned about the obstacles people would encounter along the way—and we didn't know how to address them without knowing what they all were. So we called in all

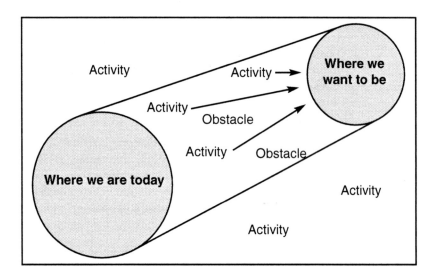

350 of the division's managers and supervisors. We explained the vision and the reality and asked the group to identify the obstacles in their way. In a month, the managers and supervisors reported back. They had uncovered 270 different obstacles. The department managers and I were stunned. Two hundred and seventy obstacles! How could we ever address all those problems and still manage to get product out the door?

"At least 30 percent of these are just perceptions," someone said. "They're not real obstacles. Maybe we could eliminate those."

"But to the people who perceive them, they're just as valid as any obstacle we're going to face," someone else argued. We agreed to deal with all 270 issues, but we would enlist some help to do it. First, we grouped the obstacles into five categories. Four categories were given back to the managers and supervisors to eradicate. The final category—the obstacles in the division directly related to culture—remained with us. As we analyzed the culture obstacles, we learned that things like autocratic leadership, functional silos, unnecessary red tape, lack of communication, and not-my-job attitudes were dragging down performance. These obstacles caused the organization to achieve significantly less than its potential. They caused work that contributed nothing to its viability. In fact, they were causing the total output of the division to be considerably less than the combined individual output of the people in it—"reverse synergy," as I would later call it.

"How can we eradicate these culture-related obstacles?" I asked.

"They all seem to be a manifestation of the negative behavior of people," someone offered.

"Right," another said. "The only way to eliminate them is to put positive behaviors in their place."

In the case of obstacles like *distrust* and *lack of respect*, the exchange was easy. *Trust* and *mutual respect* were the positive behaviors. Others were more difficult, like *shooting-the-messenger* and *not-invented-here* syndromes. But one by one, obstacles manifested by negative behavior were grouped with positive words that had the potential to eliminate them. By the time all the obstacles were organized, we had identified the following nine specific "values" we believed would eradicate negative behavior in the division:

- Trust
- Mutual Respect
- Teamwork
- Empowerment
- Risk Taking
- Sense of Urgency
- Continuous Improvement
- Commitment
- Customer Satisfaction

Reprinted courtesy of Caterpillar Inc.

We then began the process of defining each value, of developing specific behaviors to help people understand how they were expected to treat others. For example, some behaviors we developed to define Trust were *Demonstrates openness and honesty in business relationships, Does not look for or assume motives beyond those stated by others,* and *Shares information freely in all directions, both good news and bad news.*

The following weeks were filled with long days of discussion and debate as we developed specific behaviors for all of the values. We knew the "blueprint" for behavior had to be consistent, complete, and understandable for all people in our human organization. We worried about the potential for ambiguous interpretations and how that might generate conflict and stress, the very things we were trying to eradicate. It was "grunt work." There was no other word for it. Time and time again we reached consensus on how a value should be defined, and time and time again we reopened our discussions and changed the definitions. But as we worked together, a most amazing thing was happening. Not only were we defining the values, we were beginning to live them.

Instead of being forceful or loud in an effort to get our individual ways, we started to listen, really listen, to what others were trying to say. Instead of hurting feelings as sensitive issues surfaced, we began to practice real respect. We lost our need for ownership of ideas and began giving meaningful recognition to others. Our collective ideas were more innovative and powerful. What a difference we began to see! There was no question about the improved efficiency and effectiveness of our team when compared with the way we had interacted at the beginning of the values development process.

It was at this time that I began a meaningful introspection. I remembered my management style during most of my career and felt embarrassed about it. I found it difficult to believe I had progressed upward in the organization with the way I behaved as a leader. The question I struggled with was whether or not I could change and live up to the standards we would be requiring of others. I knew I had to change. I knew the worst thing that could happen was for me to introduce the values process to the organization and then not be able to walk the talk. At this point, I even considered retirement. I fully recognized the potential the process had to offer. I had witnessed it with my direct reports and was awed by it. Fortunately, I wanted to change and was determined. I wanted to be the kind of leader our vision required.

The road to change for me began with the value of Trust. My epiphany was the realization that for my entire life I had trusted no one. I had been taught not to—not purposely, but in subtle ways. Over many years, I was encouraged to write things down for the purpose of "proving" my innocence later if conflict or failure should occur. I had learned to not discuss certain things with certain people, to "spin" information to make things seem better, and to never fully admit being responsible for mistakes or failure. And I was a very good student. After struggling most of one night with what I should do, I decided to trust everyone—everyone. I decided to share what I knew without thinking of any particular motive for sharing. If I were going to get hurt from this, than hurt I would get. This decision at this moment liberated me! From then on, I saw people differently. I began to care for them and was willing to listen without judgment. Later I would see how feelings of trust would permeate our organization and would witness the power of it.

＊＊

Our Vision, Our Business Model, and *Our Common Values*—
the documents we ultimately produced—are noted on the following pages. In my four decades with the company, my most significant contribution was helping write them, living them, and creating a work environment where they were the rights and responsibilities of all people. Yes, the department managers and I had hit a home run. "Finally," I thought, "we have a road map for transforming and sustaining a positive working environment—a human organization that can drive results." I felt an exuberance welling up inside of me. I wanted to stand up and shout. We were on our way.

OUR VISION

We embrace an adaptive change culture. The only constants are the support for change and a set of common values that guide the way we manage our business. People are our competitive advantage. We work together as a single world-class team, where each has a strong desire to contribute and where decisions and behavior consistent with *Our Common Values* are recognized and rewarded. Education, training, and development are viewed as catalysts for employee and customer satisfaction and for optimizing financial results.

Reprinted courtesy of Caterpillar Inc.

OUR BUSINESS MODEL

*If we focus our leadership energies first and foremost on help-
ing people live our values, business results will improve.*

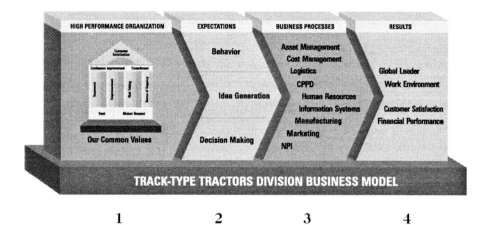

| 1 | 2 | 3 | 4 |

1. People who are required to behave in a manner consistent with *Our Common Values* are the difference between a normal and a high-performance organization.
2. Values-driven behavior generates a constant flow of un-
   constrained ideas, and synergy occurs at the most appropriate levels.
3. This causes optimum use of business processes as people work together in a values-driven environment.
4. The result is global leadership demonstrated through
   financial performance, customer satisfaction, and
   recognition as a "special place to work."

Business Model reprinted courtesy of Caterpillar Inc.

OUR COMMON VALUES

Nine building blocks interact to form the structure of *Our Common Values*. Trust and Mutual Respect are the strong foundation and starting point. Teamwork, Empowerment, Risk Taking,

and a Sense of Urgency rise out of them and give support to Continuous Improvement and Commitment. Customer Satisfaction is the peak. All Values are critical to the success of the Track-Type Tractors Division. If any value is absent, the structure is unstable and incomplete. *Our Common Values* structure is a fragile balance that depends on all people. Interaction is its strength.

> **Trust**—We believe everyone embracing the values of the division will do what is best for the customer, each other, and the enterprise.
> **Mutual Respect**—We treat everyone with dignity and courtesy.
> **Teamwork**—We recognize the potential for teams to produce superior results over what team members could achieve as individuals.
> **Empowerment**—We believe people must work in an environment where they feel enabled to make decisions that contribute to customer satisfaction and performance of the division.
> **Risk Taking**—We accept and encourage informed risk taking.
> **Sense of Urgency**—We recognize time as a competitive advantage.
> **Continuous Improvement**—We recognize everything we do as a process that can be eliminated, simplified, or improved.
> **Commitment**—We deliver what we promise to each other and to our customers.
> **Customer Satisfaction**—We delight our internal and external customers by exceeding their expectations.

> [See Appendix for complete draft of *Our Common Values* and all supporting behaviors.]

> *Our Common Values* reprinted courtesy of Caterpillar Inc.

15

A PAINFUL CONCLUSION

Leadership is action, not position.

—DONALD H. MCGANNON

We had made great progress in developing our vision and values. But one more step remained before we could unveil them to the people of our organization. For months, Gordo had continued to benchmark other companies, gathering information about their values and how they were using them in day-to-day management situations. His daughter worked at a company that used its values as its central message and primary management tool, and she shared with him their progress and the observations she had made. Through his research there and elsewhere, we began to recognize the opportunities and challenges that lay ahead. One thing in particular became clear. It was leaders— not just senior leaders, but leaders at all levels—who would need to set the example for behavior in the division. They would need to understand, support, and champion the vision and values from the very beginning. They would have to adapt—in some cases, completely change—their leadership styles to align with our values behaviors. They would have to become values role models. And they would have to do it fast.

With months of studying others, working with consultants, and the experience of developing the values behind him, Gordo volunteered to write a guidebook that would carefully define leaders' responsibilities in our new people-focused organization. His draft was then meticulously discussed, debated, and edited—first by me and then by other department managers. Finally, we approved a leadership guide that listed specific requirements and expectations for our leaders in seven key areas: developing people, fostering a positive work environment, adjusting leadership styles to meet the needs of different employees, building teams, empowering others, providing feedback, and continuously improving leadership capabilities.

The management behaviors defined by this guide would require a commitment beyond anything comprehensible at the time. It would change the overall personality of the management team to something never before witnessed by our organization. It would explicitly define our new way of leadership and require all members of management to evaluate themselves on almost 100 statements of commitment, such as *I give people freedom to handle work their own way, I listen more than I talk, I work with every employee to create a development plan,* and *I say something positive to every employee in my group every day*—simple things that we believed could make a powerful difference. Every leader would be required to read the leadership guide and say "I do" to each statement it contained. At the end of the year, all leaders would be asked to complete a survey about how well they were following these guidelines. Each leader's supervisor would fill out the same survey, and the two would meet, compare, and reach consensus on where improvement was needed. (See *Our Common Values Leadership Guide* in the appendix.)

We had drafted a new description of what leadership commitment meant in our organization. Our senior leaders—the department managers and I—were ready to make those commitments. Vision and values development had been for us a long, hard, and at times frustrating process. But it had also been a rewarding one. At first, we were merely a collection of successful, high-powered individuals, often prone to much posturing and arguing. But as time went on and we spent hundreds of hours together creating the picture of who we wanted to be, the dynamics of the group changed. We began to listen to one another. We began to change our thinking if we heard a better idea. We began to reveal who we really were and where we needed help. We became a team, consumed by the process and bound together by a vision of a better way.

We knew the change we were requiring was a significant one. The vision, values, and leadership guide we drafted defined a culture that honored people. It asked us to listen more than we talked. It required us to stop providing all the answers and let solutions come from people closest to the work. We had to relinquish control and care about others' success more than our own. Politics didn't belong here. *Who was right* wasn't important. *What was right* was. Our group had been through the process. We understood what it would take to lead this way, and we had made a commitment to do so. But we were worried about the rest of the leaders in the organization. Could they make the change from boss to coach, from commander to encourager?

"We've got to send a strong message to the organization," Gordo said. "If we tell people we expect them to behave a certain way, then allow managers to continue to behave like they always have, this is going to look like another program-of-the-month. It's not going to be fun, but we've got to take a long, hard look at those we've put in leadership positions. Can they manage in this new environment? If they don't, will all our work be for naught?"

His questions made us think. We began to look closely at our middle managers, those in the organization who made most of the day-to-day decisions. We reviewed their histories. We discussed their personalities and innate tendencies. "Is this person approachable?" we asked of every manager. "Is he or she easy to talk to and concerned with people's feelings? Do they handle conflict and disagreement well? Do they put people first?" Time after time, the answers were negative. Many of our managers had come up through the ranks and learned to lead by fear and intimidation. Most got results, sure, but they got them in spite of people, not through people. They were unpleasant people like

Frank, who raised my ire years before by cutting the doors off the bathroom stalls. Their ways of managing were so ingrained, it was hard, sometimes impossible, to imagine them ever championing and living the values.

After hours of careful consideration—and lots of brutal honesty—we came to the painful conclusion that most of our middle managers wouldn't be able to make the change as quickly as it needed to be made. We would remove them from their positions and assign them to other, non-leadership roles within the division. Managers who had the respect and trust of people would replace them.

We also came to the painful conclusion that we had too many middle managers and would reduce their number by 50 percent. Each manager that remained would have twice the responsibility and half the time to be involved in every decision their supervisors made. They would have to give decision-making responsibility back to their front-line people. And that, we were confident, would have an immediate, empowering effect on people in the division.

Reorganizing the middle-management level was a painful decision, one that seemed harsh, almost cruel. But in my heart, I knew it was the right thing to do. "We just don't have the luxury of time to wait for these middle managers to change," I thought. "Some of them never will. It's just not in their nature to lead this way." I knew how long it took us to make a new commitment and change. The department managers and I had worked for 18 months to define values, learn expectations, and adapt our leadership styles. But the division simply could not afford to wait any longer. As unfair as it seemed, there simply wasn't time for the middle managers to undergo the same extensive learning curve. The division was in crisis. Their style didn't match our new model. Change had to be fast, or the jobs and livelihoods of 4,000 employees would be in peril. If this U.S. manufacturing facility didn't achieve a fast turnaround, we faced the threat of closing plants and moving production elsewhere. "No, what we're doing may not seem fair to these middle managers," I thought. "But it is fair to the organization as a whole. We have to do what's right, what's going to make a difference for the critical mass of people here."

With that, I called the middle managers together for a meeting. I explained the vision and values, the culture change, and the new style of leadership. I explained the threats the division faced and the need to change quickly. Then I said, "Gentlemen, there is only one way for me to say what I have called you together to tell you. And that's to be as candid as I know how. Effective today, most of you are being moved to new jobs within this division, jobs that don't require you to supervise others. It's not because you haven't been effective managers in the past. It's not because you're bad people. It's because we're going on a journey to quickly change the culture in this division and we need leaders in place with different leadership styles—leaders who utilize people-based versus power-based principles. Many of you have not demonstrated those capabilities, so we are going to make some changes. For the good of this organization, for the good of the 4,000 people who work here, we are going to put leaders in place who already have skills in trusting, coaching, and encouraging people. I know this doesn't seem fair, but it's the right thing to do."

The news spread through the division like wildfire. No, most employees hadn't liked the command-and-control style of many middle managers, and they supported our decision to remove them from leadership. Still, the employees had at least known what to expect from the old managers. There had been some comfort in that stability. Now, there was change and hesitancy and fear. "What is happening?" people asked one another. "Is this fair? Is this right? Will the new people know what they are doing? Where is this heading?"

* * *

Confident as I was about the decision, even I had fears. "What if this fails? What if this fails and I have to call these people back to leadership? What if we can't run this place without them? We can forget about vision and values and culture change if that happens." Still, deep down I knew the tough decision was the right decision. I also knew the time had come to answer employees' questions about what was happening and where the division was heading. It was time to roll out the vision and Our Common Values to the entire organization.

16 THE STRUGGLE IS ON

It is morale that wins the victory.

—GEORGE C. MARSHALL*

Four days. A series of 24 all-employee meetings. One presenter. That was the way we decided to introduce the vision and *Our Common Values* to the 4,000 people in the division. "This isn't a message we can send out in a memo or an email," we said to one another. "It's important. It needs to come from the top. It needs to prove our absolute commitment to this change." So I prepared a presentation—and prepared to face every employee in the division.

I arrived at the first meeting to find the room jam-packed— 260 employees from the hourly, salaried, and management payrolls all crammed into a 220-seat auditorium, spilling into the aisles and sitting on the stage. The room was quiet as I began to

---

* George C. Marshall at Trinity College, June 15, 1941, George C. Marshall Papers, box 111, folder 3, George C. Marshall Library, Lexington, VA.

speak, first to provide a download of information on the company's business. Status quo, I'm sure many in the audience thought. Nothing different here. They kept their arms folded and their eyes on the ground. Before I was more than a few minutes into my presentation, a union committeeman seated near the back row stood up and started walking toward the door. A group of factory workers got up and began trailing behind him. I stopped speaking. The room was deadly silent. Hundreds of eyes followed the group as they proceeded to the back of the auditorium.

In a very quiet, calm voice, I broke the silence. "If you go through that door, you take significant risk."

The group stopped just short of the exit. Something in my tone made them change their minds and reverse their direction. Heads down, they returned to their seats. I immediately sensed that this was the moment to introduce *Our Common Values*. I had the entire audience's attention, and I was determined not to lose it. Pushing my papers aside, I stopped the download of business information. "Let's get right to the second part of this presentation," I said. "I want to describe the foundation of the new culture we're going to build here." I began to talk about what the business had been like over the past ten years—autocratic leadership, conflicting objectives, rigid functions. I talked about the emergence of global competition and the threat of economic recession. I talked about the solutions the division had implemented in the past—plant modernization, downsizing, reorganization. And I reminded everyone that none of these solutions had truly resolved the underlying problems.

"Employees, supervisors, managers—it doesn't matter who we are. We don't trust one another. We're not happy. We just accept the status quo. Every day, we come and do the same things, and every night we go home. There's a lack of empowerment and a lack of direction here. And we've got to change that if we're going to survive. So we're going to do two things. First, we're setting a goal to break even at the lowest point of the economic cycle. We're going to focus on the P&L as the major metric to run this business. And second, we're going to work on the human factor. We're going to create a better work environment. We're going to rediscover values and purpose, and transform our culture. And that's what I want to talk about today."

I went through the nine values and the behaviors associated with each one by one. "Everyone—management, salaried, and hourly people—is going to be expected to behave in a manner consistent with these values," I said. "When you come to work in the morning, you're expected to behave in this manner. And we will, too. I promise you that."

Then I stepped down from the stage and asked the employees sitting in chairs between the auditorium seats and the stage to move out of the way. With my foot, I drew an imaginary line on the floor.

"Do you see this line?" I challenged loudly. "Do you see it? Watch me!" I took a big step over the line. "What this means is that the management people in this place are going to take a step beyond 50 percent to make this a better place to work. And you know what? Every quarter, every quarter from now on, I will personally stand in front of you for you to grade our report card."

The auditorium had remained silent throughout the presentation—quiet enough, some said later, to hear a pin drop. But slowly, arms began to unfold. Heads began to rise. Eyes began to meet mine with expressions of hope. And after the meeting, word about *Our Common Values* spread like wildfire throughout the division. Department managers met with their employees to talk more about the values, to reinforce their commitment to this change. When all the meetings were complete, reaction from employees was cautiously optimistic. There was a feeling of hope that we were serious about changing the division.

"This is the dawn of a new age," I said to a group of department managers after the introduction. "Honest to God. Go walk through the office and the shop, and you will feel the hostility starting to drain away. You will feel it and hear it and see it on people's faces. One hundred percent? No, absolutely not. Not even 20 percent, probably. But it's visible.

"This can work. This can work. This is really going to work."

***

Despite the initial success of the vision and values introduction, we still had one major obstacle to face, a hurdle that extended far beyond our division's walls and our control. A struggle was taking place between the company and the union that represented its hourly workforce—dissention that stretched to plants and people throughout the United States. It was a conflict fought mostly with rhetoric, played out in the editorial pages and for the television cameras. It was a conflict that divided coworkers, families, and friends. It was a conflict, on the surface, over pay and benefits and job security. But deep down, it was a conflict over power and control and respect—who had it and who didn't. And neither side was willing to surrender.

Hourly workers represented by the union had gone out on strike and subsequently been locked out by the company in 1991 and 1992. By the time *Our Common Values* were introduced, workers were back on the job without a contract, and tension on the factory lines was just as intense as it had been on the picket lines. Workers literally wore their venom for the company on their sleeves—and on their hats, buttons, and jackets. At the end of each shift, they lined up at the back of the building in two huge groups. Carrying a giant American flag between them, the groups walked as a unit to the front of the plant.

"NO CONTRACT!" one side yelled.

"NO PEACE!" the other group responded.

Periodically, small one-, two-, or three-day strikes erupted—nothing major, but enough for the union to disrupt productivity and let the company know the conflict was still on. The environment reminded me of my days at the plant in Cleveland, where the workers, oppressed by plant management, conducted wildcat strikes. Despite the conflict, we proceeded with the implementation of *Our Common Values*. We continued to restructure the division's leadership team, retaining at all levels only those leaders who made—and showed—a real commitment to the values. We continued to hold meetings with all employees, where we let them ask questions about whatever was on their minds and answered them as openly and honestly as possible. We made sure values behavior expectations were clearly and consistently communicated to all employees—and when employees violated those behaviors, they were first coached on changing their behavior, then disciplined quietly and appropriately for their resulting performance when they did not. Slowly, trust in management began to elevate. Gradually, values behavior began to permeate the division.

Then, in June 1994, the union called another big strike. Factory workers were asked to walk off the job, with the goal of breaking the company's position and forcing it at last to negotiate what the union described as a "fair" contract. Much was at stake for the union and its workers, making this strike a particularly vicious one. Striking workers' disdain for the company and those hourly workers who chose to exercise their right to work (called line-crossers, or "scabs") was fierce. Crude devices called "jackrocks," consisting of two nails twisted together, were thrown onto working employees' driveways and the company's streets and parking lots, causing flat tires and fueling animosity. Hundreds of picketers guarded the gates to all the company's facilities, choking traffic and screaming obscenities at those who crossed the line. At one point, rifle shots were even fired at the homes of company management.

But the company was not about to be broken. Using a workforce of employees who exercised their right to return to work, temporary employees, retired workers, and salaried and management personnel reassigned to factory jobs, the company kept production up and continued delivering quality products to its customers. And in our division, almost 50 percent of the hourly workers, a much larger percentage than at most of the company's other plants, chose to exercise their right to work. We were confident the implementation of *Our Common Values* before the strike was the reason for it. Those hourly workers who had unfolded their arms, raised their heads, and lifted their eyes to mine when I talked to them about the values were the same hourly workers who crossed the picket lines during the strike. But they—and all the other management, salaried, and temporary employees who worked during the strike—paid a physical and emotional price to get there. Each day, they were escorted into the plant by police and security officers, pushing through an angry mob of picketers and hearing the shouts of obscenities and "Scab!" It was a frightening, often demoralizing experience— one that bonded together all the workers who entered the plant, no matter what their position or background. Like a family living in a foreign land, they turned to one another for support.

Once inside, the hatred that existed outside the factory was put aside in favor of attitudes that expressed the values. Hourly people worked side by side with office personnel who were assigned to machines that had once been operated by striking workers. They formed certification teams to improve processes. And they used the values as a guide for the strange new world in which they were working.

I often drove through the plant on a utility truck, the bed filled with doughnuts, coffee, and cool drinks that I passed out to the workers. As I did, I offered guidance and encouragement to the hourly, salaried, and management employees working together on the shop floor. All throughout the plant, I heard comments like:

"Before it was 'we' and 'them' around here, workers against the company. It seems like we're all on the same level now."

"There is less confrontation because we're all in the same boat. People are working together."

"I didn't enjoy working before. The job was boring, and no one wanted me to think. I only came for the paycheck. It's different now. My opinion matters."

The strike dragged on for more than a year. Still, the company continued to ship products from its factories at record rates, and each quarter the company's financial numbers reached new highs. Many strikers were emotionally drained from months of stress on the picket lines, coupled with increased financial insecurity. Hearing the news that the company continued to perform at its best—no, at better than its best—without them was for many the final blow. More and more workers began to cross the picket lines. Finally, in December 1995, more than 18 months after it had begun, the strike was called off by the union.

For many in the company, the end of a strike traditionally represented a victory. It meant the union position had been overcome. But I knew this time things had to be different. Again, I recalled my days at the plant in Cleveland. I remembered a similar feeling of victory after sneaking the trucks out of the plant during one of its many strikes. I remembered the company's position being overcome through tough, unyielding, forceful behavior. And I remembered the residual hurt to the organization that manifested itself into a lack of competitiveness. Several years after I left the Cleveland plant, that lack of competitiveness caused the company to shut the plant down and move production overseas.

We wanted no repeat of the Cleveland situation—no feelings of victor and vanquished, no blame, no finger pointing. "How we handle the strikers' return to our division will be a test of our commitment to the values," I said. "We cannot treat these people as prisoners of war. We have to respect the decision they made and move on. What's happened has happened. We can't change it. We've got to go forward if we are going to survive all of this, all of us together. We've got to establish a single human organization here."

As the striking workers prepared to return to the company without a contract, we spent hours preparing carefully as well. We brought in the first-line supervisors, the men and women with direct management responsibility for the hourly workforce. "We've had strikes before, and every time we say things are going to be different when they come back to work. And it never happens," one of the supervisors said. "We have to do something different this time. The plant is still the same. The machines are still the same. The tractors are still the same. Their toolboxes are still the same. So when they walk back in, everything's going to be the same unless we can show them something different."

We developed a special training program for supervisors, including role-playing sessions where they learned values-based ways to react to workers intent on disrupting the environment. Then we focused on the best way to bring the striking workers back into the workforce. The company had created a code of conduct with guidelines for behavior in its plants following the strike. At most other facilities, supervisors handed the book to the returning workers in meetings with the instruction, "Here are the rules. You better not deviate from them." We included the company's code of conduct in our return-to-work plan, but we focused on *Our Common Values*. I prepared a video describing what had gone on in the plant during the returning workers' absence and explaining what was expected of everyone in the division behaviorally—centering my message on trust, mutual respect, and the other values. The video was so important to me that I reshot it six different times. "Everything has to be perfect," I kept saying. "My body language has to be right. The words have to be exactly right, and they have to come from my heart. We can't afford to upset one person, or we'll pay a terrible price."

The video and supervisor training were completed in time for the return of the striking workers. We decided to call them back to the plant in small groups, so the values message could be presented personally to each one. "We have one shot at this, one chance to do it right," I told the first-line supervisors. "If we fail to make this work, we are letting down all the people who worked together here during the strike to support the long-term viability of our division and our company."

Supervisors called all of their employees individually, telling them what day to return to the plant and asking them to come directly to a conference room instead of reporting to their workstations. When the workers arrived, they first watched the video and then listened to their supervisor talk about *Our Common Values* and the specific behavior expectations that went along with them. "Values are a two-way street," the returning workers heard. "We're not going to allow anyone to treat you in a way inconsistent with the values. Nor will we allow you to act in a way inconsistent with the values. Acting this way is your decision. We're not going to force it on you. But this is what it's going to take to work here from now on. You can make the decision to be a part of this team, or you can make the decision not to." Of course, the workers were aware of the significant consequences that could accompany the second alternative.

At first, many of the returning workers saw the values as just one more way for the company to flex its muscles and fire them without cause. Some workers immediately tested the resolve of management by acting out and pushing the boundaries of behavior. There were outbreaks of hostility between the returning workers and those who had crossed the picket lines. Supervisors reacted calmly, as they had been trained to do, but issued quick and appropriate discipline for the manifestation of non-values behavior. They consistently reminded workers that hostility between those who had gone on strike and those who had crossed the line would not be tolerated. Most important, though, was the reaction of those who had worked in the plant during the strike. They served as "ambassadors" and role models for the returning workers. They learned to take deep breaths and bite their tongues when returning workers called them "scabs" or worse. Instead, they went out of their way to be friendly, to welcome the returning workers back to the job, to explain some of the changes that had occurred over the last 18 months, and to encourage everyone to act in ways consistent with the values. Slowly, the animosity diminished, as it became clear that the entire division was serious about the values.

One hourly worker's return to the job was of particular interest to us. Sharpe was a union committeeman—one of the highest-ranking union officials in the plant. He was also what many would have termed a "union radical." He wielded tremendous influence with his hourly coworkers, many of whom saw him as a protector. He had made it his personal agenda to protect others from the so-called abuses of management. He had stood up to us in all-employee meetings before, asking, "When is the company going to start treating us like the 20-, 25-, and 30-year employees we are—the people who made this company what it is today and made all those in leadership positions who they are? When you start treating us that way, fairly, that's when this thing will be over. Not until then." He had led many of the union demonstrations during the strike and had even been featured in *Newsweek* magazine. We were especially cautious about Sharpe's return, knowing he had the power and the influence to lead his coworkers in one of two ways: toward the values or away from them. The fact that, because of his position as union committeeman, he was one of the first to return to the plant worried us even more. When he walked back in, it was obvious his heart was still on the picket lines. Anger shone in his eyes and showed in his tensed muscles. He walked with a proud swagger as he followed his supervisors into the conference room, as if to say, "Hurry up and tell me what you're going to tell me, so I can get back to fighting."

The supervisors sat Sharpe down and began telling him about the change in the plant. "We respect your decision to do what you did," they said. "But now, we're here to do a job together, and we're going to do that job in a way consistent with these values. Trust and mutual respect are going to be the hallmarks of how we're going to operate from now on. We're going to trust you to do the right things for the business, and we expect you to trust us as well. You'll be treated with respect, and you're expected to treat others that way. We're all going to work together to make things better, not only for the company, but for the people of the company. You're not going to be fired for trying something new. You're expected to help us continuously improve. We want your ideas...."

For more than an hour, the supervisors talked to Sharpe about *Our Common Values*. As they spoke, they watched the anger drain from his body. His breathing slowed and his muscles relaxed as he leaned back in his chair, and a small smile crept onto his lips.

"Is this true? Is this really the way it's going to be—for everybody?" he asked.

"Yes, Sharpe, this is how it's going to be for everybody—you and me and every other person in this division," one of the supervisors answered.

Still cautious, Sharpe's response was merely, "We'll see." With that, he walked back into the plant. What he experienced over the next few months was an environment as different as night and day from the one he'd left more than a year and a half before. People were working together. Employees who had exercised their right to work stood side by side with workers who had shouted at them from the picket lines just months before. Many day-shift workers found ways to communicate more effectively with their night-shift counterparts. Supervisors asked employees for feedback and input. We held regular all-employee meetings, where we shared detailed information about the business—including financial results—and welcomed questions from workers. Employees were encouraged to share their ideas on ways to cut costs and better meet customer needs.

No, everything wasn't perfect. People still made mistakes, but most apologized—apologized!—for doing so. Overall, the returning workers liked the new way of doing business. They enjoyed being treated with respect. They liked having clear expectations for behavior. They responded to the challenges of continuous improvement and risk-taking. Some expressed joy, even tears, at being able to contribute for the first time, at not having to check their brains at the door when they punched the time clock and entered the plant.

"If everybody at the company behaved with *Our Common Values* in mind," one returning worker told me, "this conflict wouldn't have had so much significance in the first place."

"I've seen more things done right here in the last few months than I'd seen in my previous 25 years at this company," another offered.

But there was another opinion I wanted to hear—Sharpe's. I remembered the man's comment before the strike: "When you start treating us fairly, that's when this thing will be over. Not until then."

"Is it over with Sharpe?" I wondered.

The answer was yes. "The struggle is over. It's done," Sharpe told a coworker. "And I win. I got what I wanted. I don't have to fight anymore. I don't have to protect people anymore. I can come to work, use my hands and my brain, and make a difference. And so can everyone else."

I smiled when I heard about Sharpe's comment. "It's working," I thought. *Our Common Values* had survived their first big test.

* * *

Our job as leaders is to give people a place to work where they can be themselves, tell the truth, make meaningful decisions, and, yes, even make mistakes. I remember in grade school being afraid to read aloud in class. I was worried I'd stumble across a word I couldn't pronounce, and then I'd be laughed at. People hold back when they are afraid. Countless amounts of creativity, passion, desire, and commitment remain dormant. We had worked to create an environment where people produce amazing results because they participate actively without fear. Would we succeed?

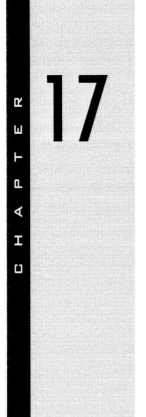

17 ONE STRONG VOICE

*When the eyes say one thing,
and the tongue another,
a practiced man relies
on the language of the first.*

—RALPH WALDO EMERSON

Gradually, as the striking workers filtered back to the plant, as things returned to normal in the division, we began to see a change in our workforce. It was subtle things, at first, that we noticed—more smiles, body language that was a bit more relaxed and open, fewer personal conflicts, in general a more positive attitude toward work and one another. So we continued with *Our Common Values* implementation. We made sure the values were communicated personally, constantly, and consistently.

"Values must be *the* central message. They must be present everywhere," I said. To help us do this I turned to Jane Converse and her firm Converse Marketing, who had been working with us throughout the process. I asked them to bring us fresh ideas and integrated plans. "First," Jane said, "we need to talk to people in the factories and offices, and learn how

Our Common Values are affecting attitudes and actions there. And to help build ownership, we need to use their words. This must be their story, not ours."

And what a story they told: "Teamwork means offering to help without being asked." "Trust is knowing the boss isn't checking on me when he stops by to talk." "Mutual Respect is when your boss isn't bossy." "Sense of urgency is doing today what you planned to do tomorrow." "Empowerment means my boss expects me to bring solutions, not problems." "Customer satisfaction is remembering the real boss around here is the person who can lay us off by buying somebody else's tractor."

We used the words of the people to create an integrated system of materials. We produced books and videos for all employees that clearly explained the values and behaviors. Large graphics and displays went up throughout all of our facilities, so everywhere employees gathered or walked, they were sure to see the values message. Our printed and electronic newsletters carried the values prominently in every issue. Even items like coffee mugs, mouse pads, and screensavers were produced with the values message. And each manager and supervisor received a small values logo lapel pin to wear every day. We wanted to make it difficult for leaders not to walk the talk.

"We've got to speak with one voice about how important our people are to our success as a division," I said. "That means we will talk about values more than we talk about profit, more than we talk about quality, more than we talk about anything."

Meetings were very important communication tools. As I had promised during the introduction, I stood up in front of the division every quarter at all-employee meetings to talk about the values and business issues. We made sure to point out results and achievements, always giving credit to the values and behaviors that people exhibited to make them happen. We didn't hide bad news, either, being just as open and honest about areas in need of improvement. And at the end of every meeting, I opened up the floor to employees. At first, many of the questions and comments I received revolved around the union–company conflict, but as time went on, they turned to issues of business—profitability, break-even, customer satisfaction, cost-cutting measures, and others. "Every single person in this organization, including the factory workers, is learning more about what's happening in our business today than I knew when I was a department manager years ago," I thought.

Even at other, more informal meetings, the values process was apparent. We made sure every conference room, every place in the division where people might meet, contained values signs—listing each of the values and their corresponding behaviors. At the end of meetings, it became common for people to ask, "How did we do on the values?" Uncomfortable as it was at the beginning, people began offering each other constructive feedback. In some meetings, people even got up and pointed to a specific value or behavior on the wall. "I don't think the decision we're making aligns with this value," they would say, or "When we interrupt one another, we're not living the value of mutual respect," and on and on and on. People who reverted to old styles of behavior were reminded gently, and in the context of the values, about their behavior. It hurt at first, but gradually people learned to give and take the criticism in a nonpersonal, nonthreatening way. They apologized for their mistakes and began to learn from them.

The same commitment to communication applied to new employees as well. Every person brought into the division was immediately introduced to the values, regardless of his or her position or length of stay. Occasionally, groups of factory workers would transfer to the division on a temporary basis to fill an immediate need. They arrived at the plant in small groups of six to 12. I personally made it a point to meet with each group individually. I handed each person a values book and said, "Welcome to our division. We're glad you're here. These are the values we live by here, and while you're with us, you're entitled to be treated in a way consistent with them. And we expect you to treat others that way too. Anytime you see someone not exhibiting these values, let your supervisor know. Or you can call me. I'm here to make sure you have a positive experience." Often, employees left these meetings fighting back tears—a few let them go. Never had they experienced such treatment from a leader, especially one at my level.

All this, I thought as I looked at the division, all this was the reason for the change in attitude. I remembered, immediately after the strike, trying to pass out quality certification plaques to hourly workers. Often, they would refuse to accept them. Once I even followed an employee halfway through the plant, just trying to get him to take a small token of appreciation. Now, however, certification recognition was a big deal. Employees proudly accepted the plaques, while their coworkers clapped, whistled, and cheered in the background. Even more remarkable, I thought, was one particular executive office presentation. Twice a year, each division in the company made a presentation to the company's executive officers—once to share the year's business plan and strategy and once to review midyear progress. A month or so before our division's presentation, we heard a group of hourly workers present a quality improvement project in a department manager meeting. We were impressed by the content and style of the presentation. "It would be so meaningful for the executive office to hear the work that our hourly people are doing as a team," I said. "Rather than us going in and talking about our culture and the results we've seen, let's show them. Let's let these hourly folks go in and give their own testimony."

I turned to the seven hourly employees involved in the presentation. "If I can get you an audience, would you be willing to present this to the executive office?" I asked.

"Yeah, sure," the group replied a bit nervously.

So I arranged for the hourly employees to deliver their presentation at the executive office review. For several weeks, they prepared carefully, each polishing his or her portion of the presentation. They even decided to wear matching shirts with the company logo. Finally, the day of the presentation arrived. We traveled to the company's headquarters and rode the elevator to the executive offices on the top floor. We stepped into the executive boardroom and looked around at the group assembled—the chairman and all the group presidents of the company. Undaunted, the hourly employees calmly delivered their quality presentation. As the last speaker stood up to talk about *Our Common Values* and the impact they had made on the process, I felt tears forming in my eyes. I felt like a proud father. As far as I knew, this was the first time hourly employees had ever made a presentation at the executive office, and they they had done an outstanding job. The change in attitudes and actions of our union represented employees was the result of all of us living our Values. I smiled as I realized that I and countless other salaried people had also changed and grown. "This is what *Our Common Values* are all about," I thought to myself.

***

But feeling good and fighting back tears wasn't what *Our Common Values* were all about, and I knew it. Sure, the change in attitude in the division was wonderful. People felt better about coming to work and working together. Worrying less about politics and policies, they were putting more effort into their jobs, enjoying them, and making a difference. But the reason we had embarked on this values journey was about more than that—it was about improving performance (financial and otherwise) in a division that was struggling. It was about hard results as much as soft ones.

I knew the results wouldn't come immediately, but I was anxious to see something concrete about the impact of the values. The first opportunity arose about a year after the values introduction, when it came time for the annual all-employee survey. The company administered this anonymous questionnaire to employees in every U.S. division. The previous year, the results from our division had lagged dramatically behind the rest of the company. I was convinced this year's survey results would show an improvement, and I waited anxiously for them to arrive. When they did, we were astounded by the numbers. We had expected improvement, yes, but these numbers were unbelievable! Employees' perception of management leadership rose by more than 30 percent. Employee identification with the division's goals jumped by over 40 percent. There was a 30 percent increase in customer focus, and a 25 percent rise in employee participation, accountability, and satisfaction. Even more impressive were the division's numbers in comparison with the rest of the company, which saw only small increases. I was ecstatic with the survey results. I made sure they were published in the division's newsletter and celebrated in all-employee meetings.

Slowly, other "hard" results began filtering in. Safety performance improved, as people were more attentive and relaxed on the job. Suppliers began to comment that the division was a different kind of organization—tough, but enjoyable to work in. They described the process of negotiating contracts, pricing, and other business issues with the division as "a meaningful experience." Customers made positive comments as well. Typically, about 12,000 to 20,000 customers visited the division each year. I led many of the tours myself and always stopped to show customers the values displays and talk about the division's culture. The response was overwhelmingly favorable. Customers liked hearing what the division stood for. They liked that I talked first about people, then about machines and quality. But what they liked most was the experience of walking through the plants. Employees stopped what they were doing to welcome the visitors—waving, smiling, and saying hello. They patiently explained their jobs and answered questions. They made a personal and powerful connection with the customers they were working so hard to satisfy.

Comments and results like these were gratifying to us. We knew *Our Common Values* were working. We could see and hear the results. But the numbers that would truly prove our case, especially to those outside the division, would arrive soon enough. Less than three years after the values introduction, our division—which had been losing tens of millions of dollars a year—showed a profit. And in less than five years, break-even (the minimum number of tractors the division had to ship a day to remain profitable) was cut by 50 percent. The results were in: The values were making a significant impact, on both the soft and the hard sides of the business.

***

Progress continued at our division over the next several years. Employee survey results continued to improve or to maintain already high levels, and the division remained profitable. *Our Common Values* remained the main emphasis, although more as reinforcement and reminders. Then, in 1998, we faced what in the past would have been considered a crisis. The year was the division's best ever profit-wise, but we soon learned that a pull-back would take place in the market over the next three years. We would not sell as many products. We would have to slow production—perhaps stop it completely at times. We would have to resort to temporary layoffs.

"Let's be careful as we start to pull back on production that we don't fall into the behaviors of the past," I told the department managers. "We want to maintain our values culture regardless of the situation we face. Above and beyond anything, we've got to preserve this culture."

In each quarterly all-employee meeting, we shared the sobering story about the business situation. Employees listened to the facts about market conditions, asked questions, and offered suggestions for cutting costs even further. Most employees saw the situation as a challenge. "How can we do things faster, more efficiently, less expensively?" they asked one another. They even came up with a motto for the situation the division faced: "As the times get tougher, the values get stronger." Eventually, the situation reached the point where several one-week plant shutdowns were necessary in order to bring production in line with market demands. In the past, temporary shutdowns raised the ire of hourly employees, whose contracts allowed for these breaks in employment. They had normally responded with angry letters to the editors of local newspapers about the unfairness of the situation. This time, however, there were no angry outbursts. Employees understood the situation the division faced and recognized that shutdowns were a last, but necessary, resort. In fact, over 200 management employees volunteered to take the time off without pay as well. They didn't think it was fair that the shutdown situation affected only the hourly workers. One management employee told me, "I really can't afford to do this, but I believe in what we're doing so deeply that I'm going to put myself on temporary layoff."

Gradually, the market began to recover. The temporary shutdowns ended, and production resumed at a higher level. We were proud of our division and our people—proud that we had remained profitable at a very low level of production, and prouder still of the way we had come together using the values in a time of crisis. The slogan was true, I thought, "As the times get tougher, the values do get stronger."

***

In spite of the ups and downs of business cycles, the hard work and dedication of our people produced year after year of improvement. My last year was no different. Our division's numbers again were better than plan: sales plus 25 percent, profit plus 50 percent, and new product quality at its highest level ever. We continue to be the best, so as I prepare to leave the company, I worry about what will happen when I am not here to light the candle of the values every day. Yet, in my heart I know—these values aren't mine and they never were. Once we agreed upon them and announced them, they belonged to the people who practiced them. Some of my proudest moments were being reminded by factory workers or others that I too needed to live the values. I learned. Others learned. We created an organization with energy and vitality. And so might you.

None of this would have been possible if Caterpillar's chairman and group presidents had not decided to make the corporation more accountable and entrepreneurial by creating independent business units and giving division executives, such as myself, profit and loss responsibility with freedom to manage our business. Out of that freedom and entrepreneurial model came Our Common Values. In the beginning, our chairman wasn't sure the values and our investment in implementing them was a good idea. He didn't see the vision for our culture as clearly as we did, but he left us alone and let us do our work. I now see that what the corporation did by transferring ownership and responsibility to our division caused this new idea called values to emerge. We were responsible for saving a division that was losing tens of millions of dollars a year. The solution came from those of us who were closest to the problem—just as innovative solutions to everyday problems often come from the people in our plants and offices, the people doing the work.

LEGACY

*The toughest thing about success
is that you have to keep on being a success.*

—IRVING BERLIN*

The year was 2001. I sat at my desk in my office in the division's headquarters, surrounded by years of memorabilia acquired during my career at the company, and thought back on the last several years. The time was about to come for my retirement, and I was reflective. I was a bit sad too. It would be a strange feeling, leaving this company where I'd worked for 43 years. Forty-three years! It was hard to imagine it had been that long.

I stepped out of my office and saw a human organization that had come so far. As I glanced at some of the familiar faces, I thought about others who had gone in new directions. No members of the original department manager team, the group that

---

* Reprinted by permission of the Estate of Irving Berlin.

had painstakingly crafted the vision and values, remained. Many had gone on to other positions in the company. Gordo was retired. Others were leading plants and divisions. I had been sad to see them leave, but I also felt a sense of pride that the company respected our division's people enough to promote them on to bigger and better things. I was proud of teaching, encouraging, coaching, and growing people for more responsible and successful careers. And I was most proud of the fact that many of these leaders had taken the values message with them on their journey through the company.

There was the plant in North Carolina, for example, led by one of my management employees. "Now there's a success story," I thought. The facility was part of my division and had been purchased in 1996. Back then, there was a lot of distrust between employees and management. With our help, the new managers carefully implemented *Our Common Values,* using the same techniques the department managers and I had used a few years before—removing leaders who couldn't lead in a values-driven way, making values the central message of all communications, consistently rewarding and recognizing those who exhibited values behavior. They even adopted our business model, which said the way to create a high-performance organization was to focus on people with values, who in turn deliver results. The change in the North Carolina facility was dramatic. Employees began to trust management and knew management trusted them. Today, it was clear why the North Carolina plant was profitable and its employee survey results were outstanding—just as high as our facilities back in Illinois.

And then there was the plant in China—an even more remarkable story, I realized as I thought about the situation. One of my former department managers, Mark, had been named the plant manager of this facility a few years earlier. It was a relatively small business just getting started then, manufacturing hydraulic excavators, and losing several million dollars a year. The plant was staffed entirely by Chinese nationals, except for a few management people brought over from the United States. The technical capabilities of the employees were quite adequate, but the plant's culture and vision for the future were lacking. Within 60 days of his arrival, Mark brought the idea of values to the organization.

He and his new management team made an outline of expectations for behavior, then put together a team of people from all over the facility to define values and behaviors. The list ended up almost identical to the one our team had developed.

At first, many people doubted that American words and concepts like trust and risk taking could be implemented in such a different culture. How, people asked, in a country where unique business practices by U.S. standards are a part of everyday work, can a company expect its employees to behave differently? How can they be expected to trust others when their management controls rather than trusts its people? How can they be encouraged to think for themselves when those who express new ideas or take risks face severe penalty? I remembered Mark's explanation to the employees at the plant: "When we walk through the doors of this facility, we're not American or Chinese anymore—we're our own culture with our own set of expectations. We're all members of this organization, and as long as we behave in a manner consistent with our values, we will always be supported by this organization."

And he was right, I thought proudly. The values were fully implemented at the Chinese plant. People were expressing ideas, trying new things, trusting their coworkers and management. They were also producing results. The plant had begun to turn a modest profit and had even been featured in a *Fortune* magazine article about the changes taking place in China. Values, it seemed to me, were working all over the world. But there were success stories closer to home, too. Other former department managers now at the company's headquarters were implementing values there as well. I could see improvements, many of the same improvements I'd seen in our own division. It was gratifying to see other leaders beginning to realize that the only way to achieve success in perpetuity was by inspiring and empowering people. It was rewarding to see technology advancements and process improvements come as a result of cultures that celebrated people and assured that they were engaged to the fullest in their work.

Still, there was work to be done. Too many leaders still saw values as something soft, words to place on a wall or put in a book and refer to every now and then. I shook my head. I knew from experience that values were anything but soft. Sure, they gave you guidelines for treating people with trust and respect, but they also dealt with hard performance issues like commitment to responsibility, continuously improving, taking risks, and satisfying customers. Values set high standards for performance. They also set requirements for leaders: Communicate expectations consistently. Reward and recognize those who meet or exceed them. Coach those who do not. And remove those who, after coaching, cannot live up to expectations. For too long, I had realized years ago, our division had spent most of its time focusing on the poor performers—a group amounting to just 5 percent of the workforce. But now, with values and behavior expectations in place, leaders were able to spend most of their time focusing on the 95 percent of people who were performing well—recognizing them, encouraging them, challenging them to do more. That was right. That was fair. That was the way it should be.

"Management is starting to develop the intestinal fortitude to deal with substandard performance," I said to myself. "In the past, we were all reluctant to deal with people who didn't carry their load, but we found we had to. We owed it to those people who did perform, who did excel. If we hadn't dealt with poor performers, we would have let the rest of the organization down."

These are lessons, I thought, we took too much time to learn.

***

Later that day, I attended a meeting at one of the division's other facilities. Afterward, I walked around the shop floor for a while, stopping to chat with the workers and reflecting on my own days in the plant many, many years before. I ran into Sharpe, the union radical who had given us so much trouble in the days before the big strike. Sharpe was now a management employee. He'd been recommended for a supervisory position, took the division's leadership assessment test, and was now a first-line supervisor—using *Our Common Values* to lead, guide, coach, and reward his own employees. In fact, I remembered as I looked around, Sharpe was just one of at least five former striking workers now in management positions within the division.

Times sure have changed, I thought. Forty-three years ago when I first stepped onto the shop floor, there was little thought of moving up to a "company job." You worked your shift. You did just what it took to get by. Do less, and you got in trouble with the boss. Do more, and you got in bigger trouble with the boys on the line. But I had learned a lot on the shop floor. I remembered Duggan, my instructor in the apprentice program who had been so kind when I hurt my eye. Treating employees with kindness, getting to know and respect them as people, not just workers, was the lesson Duggan had taught me. I remembered Howard, known as one of the meanest, toughest supervisors in the company, who in his own way encouraged and rewarded me for my hard work. I remembered how much I had wanted to achieve for Howard. That was another lesson I'd carried with me throughout my career.

But I had learned some negative lessons in the plant, too. There were behaviors I'd seen—and many I'd even used myself—that I'd had to learn not to replicate. Like the time I was laid off for running scrap—that was punishment for taking a risk. Then, I had learned the lesson, "Break the rules. Pay the price." But now I knew there was more to it than that. Now I knew how important it was to encourage people to take informed risks, to take on challenges and learn from mistakes. How could people achieve great things if they were afraid to take the chance? Then there were the times I hadn't been rewarded for doing a good job. There was my supervisor, Big Stan, who liked my hard work so much he refused to promote me. There was my boss at the small tool and die shop who wouldn't give me the commission promised. Again, I'd learned a negative lesson. Why go above and beyond the call of duty if there's never going to be a reward? Why try harder? Why exceed expectations? Fortunately, something in my character never allowed that to happen. Something inside me that couldn't be defeated made me always want to try harder, work faster, do it better. But I'd seen many others beaten down by the negative lessons they'd learned on the job. During my 43 years at the company, I'd seen hundreds—maybe thousands—of talented employees, employees with skills and intelligence and capability, who'd never used them to the fullest. It just wasn't expected, wasn't encouraged, and perhaps wasn't even wanted by those who managed them.

"Maybe that's why I'm different," I said aloud, struck by the thought. "Because I was there. Because I came up through the ranks. Because I started at the lowest level on the shop floor and I worked my way up for years and years. I saw so many people with so much capability, and I saw so little of it ever used. And I saw what that did to people. It made some angry and lash out at the company. It made some indifferent and uncaring about the company's success. It made everyone feel a little less important, a little less worthwhile. And that held the company back. Sure, we've been successful, but how much more successful could we have been if we'd only unleashed the power of all those people? How much more could we have achieved?"

***

Stepping out of my reverie, I looked around at the plant in which I stood. I saw people working together. I saw smiles and laughter. And I saw products going out the door. Somehow, I had learned from the lessons of the past, and so had those I worked with in the division. We'd taken the good and built on it, taken the bad and made it good. And we'd learned the most important lessons of all: that people are basically good and, given the right environment, want to contribute, make a difference, and satisfy the expectations placed on them. That people mirror the behavior they see exhibited and rewarded. That leaders have tremendous responsibility to exhibit the behavior they want to see in their people. So we had decided to paint a picture of the behavior we wanted to see. We decided to put ourselves in front of a mirror and ensure the reflection was one we were proud of. We established values and behaviors as the ground rules for working together—not to change people for the sake of change, but to channel their diversity and unleash their creativity in a way that works for the good of all individuals and the organization as a whole.

Values-based leadership had worked, was working, would continue to work, I was convinced, as long as people—leaders and followers—made a commitment to making it work. So many people had changed so dramatically, including me. There is no way to go back to the people I had dealt with inappropriately or unfairly along the way. I can't go back, but I can offer my story as an apology to them. I hope this book reveals that their experiences with me helped me find a better way to lead. My only regret is that I did not discover the values process sooner.

Yes, I was humbled, but also I was proud. I was proud to have helped develop a place where people could truly be themselves and, as a result, achieve great things individually and for the company. I was proud of my own transition, from a somewhat conflicted manager trying to incorporate the mixed messages I received through the years, to a strong leader living and leading consistently with *Our Common Values*. And I was proud of each person in our division who had taken the values journey with me. "This is my story, but as I look at the thousands of people around me, I realize they've all taken a journey too," I thought, "and each one of them has a story as profound as mine to tell.

"It's been one hell of a ride. It really has."

19 THE LEGACY LIVES

We cannot live only for ourselves. A thousand
fibers connect us with our fellow-men;
and along those fibers, as sympathetic threads,
our actions run as causes, and they come back to
us as effects.

—HERMAN MELVILLE

oes an environment of dignity make a difference in the lives of people? In the performance of a business? I know it does. I saw it in the hearts of those who worked with me in the offices and factories at Caterpillar. And I saw it in the results they produced every day. Below are some stories told by those who took the values journey with me. Yes, the legacy lives on through them; but, as importantly, when you embrace the values-based leadership processes and principles documented in this book, the legacy lives on through you.

The facility in China was having financial difficulties when I moved here as plant manager. Our first priority was turning the business around. Looking back, if I hadn't lived through the values process in Jim's division, I probably would have started by attacking what we always attack, and that is technology. I most likely would have missed the opportunity to unleash the talent of our Chinese employees. We would have figured out a way to make technically good products, because this company always manages to make the best product one way or another. But we wouldn't have done it with the enthusiasm or the profitability or the true pride of workmanship our people have in our products. These are all the results of the trust we have given our employees and the investment we have made in them as part of this values process.

—Mark McDaniel, former General Manager of Xuzhou (People's Republic of China) Operations, now Director General of Mexican Operations, Caterpillar Inc.

As a result of my experience in Jim's division, I'm more open. I'm much faster to engage my organization today and recognize that the solution to a problem may lie with my group, outside of me. It's interesting that there have been a lot of false starts with values. In other words, people go to a two-day offsite and come back with a values statement or pyramid or whatever. They announce it to the organization, maybe even go so far as to draw up a leadership guide, but then it just sits there. There's not the leadership. There's not the follow-up. There's not the prominence of values on a day-to-day basis that there is in the tractors' division. Values can either be background, a kind of corporate Muzak if you will, or they can be symphony. They need to be symphony if they're going to drive results.

—Rich Lavin, former Product Manager, now Vice President of Corporate Human Services Division, Caterpillar Inc.

When I first hired in to this company, I worked under fear. When I became a supervisor, I thought my job was to be an autocrat. That's how I got raises. It was either my way or out the door, and I was very good at it. Everybody knew my reputation. That pretty much was the way we all operated before the day Jim told us that we were going to do something different. He told us about *Our Common Values* and a different type of managing style. I don't think any of us knew what Jim was talking about. We were laughing and thinking it was just another program that would hit the road. But pretty soon we began to realize, hey, this is for real. Jim was serious. So I grabbed my leadership guide and read it from cover to cover. I knew I had a long way to go. I probably was one of those people they didn't believe would ever make the change, but I did. I still have work to do on supporting the values every day, though; it's easy to slip back. I knew I was on the right road when I met a woman at a wedding reception whose friend worked for me. She told me he was happy because he was on a team and making decisions—he was the happiest he'd ever been at this company.

> —*Bob Zimbelman, First Line Supervisor,*
> *Caterpillar Inc., retired*

By far, *Our Common Values* are the best thing that has happened to the hourly workforce that I have seen in my years here. The very best. We've had a lot of programs come and go, a lot of "get along" programs and a lot of let-downs over the years. This values process is something that everyone in the shop is proud of. We come to work now and we don't have to check our brains at the gate. We share information and receive information about our business—how things are going, what we need to change to improve profit. We talk about costs all the time. We're asked for our ideas on how to save money. It's so different from my days in the shop years ago. In the building where I work right now, there are at least five of us in management who were hired off the shop floor. Jim gave us the opportunity to use the values to make a difference. Four of us are people who were once out on strike. You won't find many companies doing that—giving management responsibility to former strikers, including me, who was a union leader. So I say there's one of two things going on here. Either whoever's in charge of this company is totally nuts or these values really make a difference. And the answer is, the values make a difference.

—Jim Sharpe, former Union Committeeman, now Operations Supervisor, Caterpillar Inc.

I truly believe that the values are going to go down in history as a defining moment for our corporation. We have shown that you can turn attitudes and financials around in very short order if you are serious about it. We bought this manufacturing facility in North Carolina from an outside supplier in 1996. Three years later, our performance had totally turned around. You can point to one thing that caused that to happen, and that is the values. We found we could work together as employees and management with trust, mutual respect, and teamwork. The values culture has totally transformed this small facility in the mountains of North Carolina. We are far away from headquarters, but the impact of the values is so strong that it has just totally changed this place. I feel blessed not only that was I in Jim's division, but that I had a chance to work for him directly. Other than my family, no other person in my life has made me grow and learn more than he has.

—Jon Harrison, former Undercarriage Business Manager, now Facility Manager, Caterpillar Precision Seals, Franklin, North Carolina

If I go back to what made everybody in East Peoria really think that the values process was meaningful, it was the willingness to "bite the bullet" and make the hard personnel decisions right up front—to recognize that there are certain people who just won't or can't operate this way. You need absolute commitment, leadership focus, passion, and heart from the top. That is what will make it happen. Who was it who burned all the ships in Mexico?

I think it was Cortez. He burned all the ships and said, "We're going to conquer Mexico. There are no other options, this is what's going to happen." You almost have to take the same approach with values. Anything else is half measures and perceived as such.

—*Greg Folley, former Human Relations Manager, now Director of Corporate Compensation and Benefits, Caterpillar Inc.*

I am a passionate believer in the values process and was an ardent supporter of Jim in our values journey. In my judgment, the process was the pinnacle in the transformation and growth of Jim—in his moving from a manager to a true leader. By integrating his passion and dedication for the values with his many personal attributes and managerial experience, Jim was able to lead our division through a remarkable turnaround in employee attitude and morale, accompanied by outstanding financial results. Some of our values had been a part of the company's writings for some time, but Trust, Mutual Respect, Sense of Urgency, and Risk Taking were given lip service at best. The explicit statement and definitions of the nine values and accompanying norms of behavior were powerful. But standing by themselves, they were just another placard on the wall. They became credible and powerful because of the full court press put on by Jim and the senior leaders. By ensuring that everything we did was in alignment with the values, the leader group established and preserved a work environment that unleashed the power of the people at all levels. It resulted in numerous breakthroughs in many areas, both in operations and the office. It propelled us to outstanding achievements in product development, global leadership, customer satisfaction, employee satisfaction, and financial performance. One has to take deep satisfaction in taking part in a process that makes a difference in the lives of your associates at work—

with that difference culminating in outstanding results. It was fun and a joy to be part of this transformation.

—Bob "Gordo" Gordon, Product Manager,
Caterpillar Inc., retired

I met Jim in 1993 when our company was asked to be the "communication player" on his culture change team. Like many who participated in this amazing process, we watched "dignity for all" work its magic. Like a tiny pebble rolling down a mountain, it started slowly and then grew huge and powerful as it collected the will and the energy of people. We watched values become a "force field" around an entire organization, giving people noble standards for their behavior and amazing freedom to be themselves. Was this a story about Jim? Yes. But it is also about you and me. It is a lesson in leadership for those of us who are honest enough to see ourselves in his journey from control-based to values-based leadership—and smart enough to want to follow his path to change.

—Jane Converse, co-author of this book;
president of Converse Marketing, communication
professionals; and a partner in DespainConverse,
values-based leadership consultants

CONCLUSION

My life, like others' lives, has been a series of experiences that shape my interpretation of things around me. It is impossible to know the total impact of one's life experiences—how they affect proactive and reactive behavior, for example. But in my mind, one thing is certain: I would not have recognized the potential of the values process or supported its development and ultimate use without the life experiences shared in this book. No one came forth to teach me the "good" in putting people first, trusting them, empowering them, and caring for them. And if someone had, I would have strongly resisted their teaching without hard evidence of material benefit to the company. I was driven—driven to succeed—and would have stayed with traditional, tested ways. I would have concluded that a "values-based" approach was a weak person's answer to the challenge we were facing, and I would have killed it in its infancy. But as we explored the new process, something inside me connected with the lessons learned throughout my life. Values made sense to me, and I became passionate about them.

As our leader group explored the idea and began to trust one another, many ideas surfaced that made a difference. We started a 360-degree feedback process that made leaders aware of how others perceived their behaviors—as consistent or inconsistent with expectations. We made feedback private, personal, and disconnected from the performance evaluation process and pay. Workers' evaluations were also based on values behavior rather than company results. Not surprisingly, when thousands of people started exhibiting trust, mutual respect, sense of urgency, risk taking, empowerment, teamwork, commitment, continuous improvement, and customer satisfaction, we consistently achieved our goals and drove outstanding company results.

Over the years we proved, without a doubt, that the right behavior produces the right results. I remember years ago when we as leaders spent our time focusing on *things* like manufacturing processes to make product quality better—the better and more consistent the manufacturing process, the better and more consistent product quality. Today our leaders focus on *people*, and the people make product quality better. Values-based leadership is also a process—a human process. The better and more consistent the values-based leadership process is, the better and more consistent are the organization's results.

So why hasn't every part of our company, or all companies for that matter, adopted this process? Is it because it is someone else's idea, the *Not Invented Here Syndrome*? I don't think so. I believe it is very difficult to change our traditional or historical approach to management, to give up the "power of office," so to speak. Managers too often are "control freaks," more confident of themselves than they are of the people they serve. Trusting others is uncomfortable for many—an upside down idea. But think about what happened to us. We succeeded because we had an entire organization of people as connected to the company's success as the one at the top. A single manager or management group is no match for an army of committed people in a culture that treats them with dignity and builds their self-worth.

In closing, I'd like to put to rest the notion that the values-based leadership process is a "soft" approach. It's one of the toughest, hardest things I ever did. And the most rewarding. We worked tirelessly to help people stretch to reach their maximum potential and saw their human dignity and energy enhanced. I share my story to help you unlock the unlimited potential of your human organization. And when shared values are owned by your people, you too can expect unbelievable, sustainable performance and the personal joy it brings.

APPENDIX

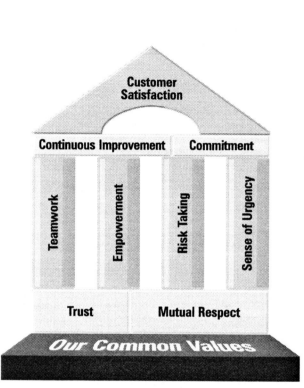

* Reprinted courtesy of Caterpillar Inc.

OUR COMMON VALUES

Trust—We believe everyone embracing the values of the division will do what is best for the customer, each other, and the enterprise.

- Acts consistently to reinforce our values.
- Expects people to perform their mission and be accountable.
- Demonstrates openness and honesty in business relationships.

- Eliminates the fear of breaking away from familiar ways of thinking and acting.
- Shares information freely in all directions, both good news and bad news.
- Does not look for or assume motives beyond those stated by others.
- Respects and honors matters of confidentiality.

Mutual Respect—We treat everyone with dignity and courtesy.

- Makes everyone feel important and able to make a contribution.
- Listens without interruption when someone is speaking.
- Makes no distinction based on position.
- Accepts or gives apologies when appropriate.
- Recognizes the uniqueness of individuals.

Teamwork—We recognize the potential for teams to produce superior results over what team members could achieve as individuals.

- Believes that teaming is the balanced involvement of all relevant functions.
- Aligns personal work and team activities to optimize contribution to the division.
- Accepts and supports team decisions after individual views have been expressed.
- Resolves disagreements within and between work teams by doing what is best for the enterprise.
- Contributes to the success of others by helping others solve problems, meet deadlines, and work effectively.
- Openly shares relevant information.

Empowerment—We believe people must work in an environment where they feel enabled to make decisions that contribute to customer satisfaction and performance of the division.

- Defines the boundaries of accountability and freedom to act, but remains flexible to meet changing business needs.
- Balances decision-making authority and responsibility.

- Drives decision-making authority and responsibility to the lowest level of competency.
- Seeks and shares information with others on decisions that affect them.
- Provides opportunities for employees to develop new skills, expertise, and perspective.
- Understands how individual work impacts the division's success.
- Develops the capability of others through active mentoring and coaching.

Risk Taking—We accept and encourage informed risk taking.

- Nurtures risk taking in the workplace.
- Recognizes failures associated with reasonable risk taking should not be punished but used as an opportunity for improvement to the underlying processes.
- Demonstrates the courage to speak freely and challenges the status quo to stimulate change and make decisions to move us forward.
- Challenges prescribed methods and procedures to better serve the customer.
- Recognizes the real risk to business success lies in not challenging and improving processes.
- Offers recognition for informed risk taking.

Sense of Urgency—We recognize time as a competitive advantage.

- Places a high priority on time. Delivers work on time to both internal and external customers.
- Works to reduce time required to perform assigned tasks. Removes needless steps.
- Errs in the direction of moving too fast rather than moving too slow.
- Acts quickly to accomplish our goals and meet our commitments.
- Assesses the situation and acts accordingly.

- Responds to questions and issues immediately or as soon as appropriate information is collected.

Continuous Improvement—We recognize everything we do as a process that can be eliminated, simplified, or improved.

- Asks "How can it be improved?" rather than "Does it need to be improved?"
- Recognizes the value of change for improvement.
- Focuses on problem prevention rather than problem resolution.
- Evaluates changing technology and optimizes its use.
- Recognizes redundancy and waste must be eliminated.
- Eliminates unneeded processes (practices/systems) without concern for impact on specific job assignments.
- Accepts self-development as a process that needs continuous improvement.
- Recognizes processes as the key to performance improvement.
- Makes decisions based on need or opportunity, not precedent.

Commitment—We deliver what we promise to each other and to our customers.

- Recognizes action rather than rhetoric as the true measure of commitment.
- Promises only what can be delivered.
- Demonstrates personal commitment to continued learning and upgrading of skills.
- Communicates the impact of change to base assumptions used to make commitments.
- Accepts obligation to continuous improvement.

Customer Satisfaction—We delight our internal and external customers by exceeding their expectations.

- Listens to customers.
- Actively solicits input from customers for important decisions. Always assumes the customer has something to contribute.

- Always asks, "How can I better serve the customer?"
- Responds with urgency to customers' feedback, including both complaints and suggestions.
- Delights the customer with quality and service that exceeds competition. Increases customer loyalty to our products by always providing support.
- Effectively represents the interests of the customer. Is willing to "go to bat" for customers.

*Our Common Values reprinted courtesy of Caterpillar Inc.

OUR COMMON VALUES LEADERSHIP GUIDE

A guide that examines seven key leadership responsibilities and explains how we carry them out in a manner that supports *Our Common Values*.

1. **Develop people to their fullest capacity**
   - I have a clear vision of what constitutes growth for the people I serve.
   - I work with employees to create written development plans.
   - I help employees master the skills they need to succeed on the job.
   - I give people freedom to handle work their own way.
   - I take time to show employees new ways of doing work.
   - I delegate assignments to help people stretch or broaden their skills.
   - I accept mistakes as part of the development process and help people avoid repeating mistakes in the future.
   - I discuss career goals with each employee.
   - I provide honest, realistic answers to career questions and never make promises I cannot keep.

- I help people understand the skill requirements and selection criteria for other jobs.
- I encourage employees to take advantage of internal and external education and training opportunities.
- I encourage people to make lateral moves to broaden their knowledge of the organization.
- I reward and celebrate developmental achievements.
- I set an example for others by visibly pursuing a self-development plan.

2. **Foster a positive work environment**

- I have a positive outlook.
- I believe it is my job to help people succeed.
- I believe that people want to work hard, do their best, and make a useful contribution.
- I am friendly and courteous to everyone.
- I say "thank you" to employees throughout the day.
- I look people in the eye when I talk to them.
- I call employees by their names.
- I keep my promises.
- I accept criticism.
- I admit when I'm wrong.
- I ask for help.
- I give credit for good ideas.
- I listen more than I talk.
- I maintain a harassment-free work area.
- I set high standards for quality, performance, and behavior, and hold people accountable to these standards.
- I provide people with as much information as I can about our company, our division, Cat products, competition, and other vital issues.
- I help employees understand the value of the contributions they make. I talk with employees about their families, hobbies, interests, and outside activities.
- I encourage people to have fun at work.

3. **Adjust leadership style to meet the needs of those whom we serve**

    ■ I understand the four basic leadership styles: directing, coaching, supporting, and delegating.

    ■ I assess the competency level of each employee on my team.

    ■ I assess the commitment level of each employee on my team.

    ■ I use different leadership styles with different people.

    ■ I use different leadership styles with the same person, depending on their competency and commitment to a given task.

    ■ I change leadership styles as an employee's or team's competency and commitment levels change.

4. **Build and support committed and effective teams**

    ■ I understand the goals of our company, our division, and our work group, and I have communicated them clearly to employees.

    ■ I appreciate the unique background, skills, and perspective each employee contributes to the team.

    ■ I use the collective talent and expertise of the people on my team.

    ■ I help all employees understand their respective roles on our team.

    ■ I remind employees of our team goals.

    ■ I explain how our team's results affect the entire division.

    ■ I work at building positive relationships among team members.

    ■ I encourage open communication on the team.

    ■ I encourage team members to share responsibility for team leadership.

    ■ I praise individual and team accomplishments and celebrate successes.

    ■ I share responsibility for winning and losing.

    ■ I support my team whether we are winning or losing.

- I discourage behavior that weakens team morale and performance.
- I encourage employees to serve on multifunctional teams.
- I set an example for others by serving on multifunctional teams.

5. **Empower others to serve internal and external customers**

- I keep people informed about the issues that affect the work group.
- I solicit input from employees on decisions that affect them.
- I provide as much information as I can about the work group, the division, and the company.
- I explain how every individual's work affects the organization's success.
- I challenge people to learn continuously.
- I ask for ideas and advice.
- I remove roadblocks.
- I provide appropriate resources to get a job done.
- I expect and encourage people to manage their own responsibilities and find their own solutions.
- I trust people to make good decisions without my help.
- I accept and support team decisions that are not made the way I would have made them.
- I allow people to fail, but assure that the failure is not devastating to the person or the organization.
- I provide adequate and appropriate training.

6. **Provide feedback that helps people grow**

Developmental feedback

- I work with every employee to create a development plan.
- I give positive feedback when employees show developmental progress.

- I modify employees' development plans as they reach their goals.
- I give developmental feedback and performance appraisals at separate times.
- I give developmental feedback more than once a year.
- I ask for employee input in my personal development plan.

Informal feedback

- I say something positive to every employee in my group every day.
- I identify attitudes or behaviors that I would like to perpetuate.
- I look for opportunities to reward behavior and performance consistent with *Our Common Values*.
- I strive to reinforce positive behavior immediately after it happens.
- I praise employees for specific behaviors or achievements.
- I give positive reinforcement for everyday work effort—not just exceptional performances.

Disciplinary feedback

- I apply discipline consistently.
- I meet privately with employees to discuss problems.
- I try to resolve problems before they enter the formal disciplinary process.
- I explain to employees what constitutes reasonable performance and behavior.
- I tell employees why expected levels of performance and behavior are essential to our team.
- I let people know when their performance or behavior is not meeting expectations.
- I explain what needs to be done to bring performance or behavior to acceptable levels.
- I try to get employees to accept responsibility for changing their behavior.
- I seek the employee's agreement to resolve the problem.

- I work with the employee to create an action plan for resolving the problem.
- I clearly state the consequences of failing to meet expectations.

7. **Pursue self-development**

- I have a written plan for self-development.
- I discuss personal developmental issues with coworkers at all levels of the organization.
- I meet regularly with my supervisor to talk about developmental opportunities and progress.
- I seek out new responsibilities and new approaches to problem solving.
- I take advantage of internal and external education and training activities.
- I accept lateral moves and cross-training assignments.
- I use the 360-Degree Values Feedback Process to guide my development plans.
- I take advantage of the Division Leadership Upward Feedback Process.

Our Common Values Leadership Guide reprinted courtesy of Caterpillar Inc.

8 reasons why you should read the Financial Times for 4 weeks RISK-FREE!

To help you stay current with significant
developments in the world economy ...
and to assist you to make informed business
decisions — the Financial Times brings you:

 Fast, meaningful overviews of international affairs ... plus daily briefings on major world news.

 Perceptive coverage of economic, business, financial and political developments with special focus on emerging markets.

 More international business news than any other publication.

 Sophisticated financial analysis and commentary on world market activity plus stock quotes from over 30 countries.

 Reports on international companies and a section on global investing.

 Specialized pages on management, marketing, advertising and technological innovations from all parts of the world.

❼ Highly valued single-topic special reports (over 200 annually) on countries, industries, investment opportunities, technology and more.

❽ The Saturday Weekend FT section — a globetrotter's guide to leisure-time activities around the world: the arts, fine dining, travel, sports and more.

FT FINANCIAL TIMES
World business newspaper

The *Financial Times* delivers a world of business news.

Use the Risk-Free Trial Voucher below!

To stay ahead in today's business world you need to be well-informed on a daily basis. And not just on the national level. You need a news source that closely monitors the entire world of business, and then delivers it in a concise, quick-read format.

With the *Financial Times* you get the major stories from every region of the world. Reports found nowhere else. You get business, management, politics, economics, technology and more.

Now you can try the *Financial Times* for 4 weeks, absolutely risk free. And better yet, if you wish to continue receiving the *Financial Times* you'll get great savings off the regular subscription rate. Just use the voucher below.

Where to find tomorrow's best business and technology ideas. TODAY.

- Ideas for defining tomorrow's competitive strategies — and executing them.

- Ideas that reflect a profound understanding of today's global business realities.

- Ideas that will help you achieve unprecedented customer and enterprise value.

- Ideas that illuminate the powerful new connections between business and technology.

ONE PUBLISHER.
Financial Times Prentice Hall.

 Prentice Hall
FINANCIAL TIMES

WORLD BUSINESS PUBLISHER

AND 3 GREAT WEB SITES:

Business-minds.com

Where the thought leaders of the business world gather to share key ideas, techniques, resources — and inspiration.

InformIt.com

Your link to today's top business and technology experts: new content, practical solutions, and the world's best online training.

ft-ph.com

Fast access to all Financial Times Prentice Hall business books currently available.